T0146933

COME AND GO WITH ME

A Collection of Stories and Lessons

MARTHE CURRY, Ph.D.

Illustrations by Brenda Kingery
with Barry Watson, *and* Threads of Blessing

WESTBOW
PRESS®
A DIVISION OF THOMAS NELSON
& ZONDERVAN

WestBow Press books may be ordered through booksellers or by contacting:

WestBow Press
A Division of Thomas Nelson & Zondervan
1663 Liberty Drive
Bloomington, IN 47403
www.westbowpress.com
844-714-3454

ISBN: 979-8-3850-0778-3 (sc)
ISBN: 979-8-3850-0777-6 (e)

Print information available on the last page.

WestBow Press rev. date: 09/28/2023

To my children,
my grandchildren,
and the people of the Episcopal Diocese of West Texas.

"There's no sense in going further—it's the edge of cultivation,"
So they said, and I believed it—broke
my land and sowed my crop—
Built my barns and strung my fences in the little border station
Tucked away below the foothills where the trails run out and stop.
Till a voice, as bad as conscience, rang interminable changes
On one everlasting whisper day and night repeated—so:
"Something hidden. Go and find it. Go
and look behind the Ranges—
"Something lost behind the Ranges. Lost
and waiting for you. Go!"
And "no sense in going further"—till I crossed the range to see ...
Anybody might have found it but—His whisper came to me!
—Rudyard Kipling, *The Explorer*, 1898

CONTENTS

3. Stumbling Around

4. Fellow Travelers

5. On the Road

INTRODUCTION

"Come and go with me to my Father's house," was the raucous chorus we shouted through children's chapel every Friday night at the little community church. There were numberless verses, each one ending with, "There is joy, joy, joy!"

Growing up in a home where Bible reading and prayer began and ended each day, it's no wonder that I gravitated to ministry early on. When my brother Jack was four and I was six, we sang our first duet in church. My Sunday school teacher invited me to be her assistant when I was in primary school, and I eventually taught Bible studies and wrote short devotionals.

I married early and had two beautiful children, but, unexpectedly, our family fell apart, and I was on my own for the first time. It was difficult, as any single parent will testify, but the hardships merely served as nudges for spiritual growth. The children and I learned to depend on the Lord and to accept the provisions he often sent as surprises of love.

Fourteen years after divorce, with myriad challenges and victories, I married Peter, a widower who would bring healing and inspiration to the three of us. Teaching and music were givens, but ministry expanded when my husband and I had the privilege of caring for two grandsons, a teenager, and a toddler. Peter, a judge, touched lives daily as he dispensed mercy and law, with stories of God's grace often flowing from his courtroom.

Blessed with many rich experiences of God's faithfulness, I was asked to write a blog encouraging readers to continue pursuing deeper faith in a loving Father and his Son, Jesus Christ. The blog inspired this collection. In *Come and Go with Me*, friends and I share real-life happenings along with excerpts from literature about a God who is always there.

Years of mission vocation are noted in each section, while other tales are part of daily plodding. Included are spaces for reflection with prompts for walking Christ's narrow way.

The stories here are organized by guideposts, starting with section 1, *The Call*, to provide a map of sorts beginning with the manner by which we discern God's direction for us personally.

Section 2, *Getting Ready,* suggests steps in spiritual growth that help us move away from transactional religion toward a growing personal relationship with God. It's quite likely that most of us will have experienced times of *Stumbling Around* (section 3) in pursuit of sainthood. Through these pages, we'll see that bumps are just part of the journey and are no reason to turn back.

Ideally, *Fellow Travelers* (section 4) walk with us when the road is rough and stay around to sing when we celebrate. There are times, however, when we feel alone on the road and can barely put one foot ahead of the other. That's when we especially appreciate the unseen presence of our faithful Lord who sustains us to our destination.

While *On the Road* (section 5), God moves among us calling us to himself, and in responding, we find ourselves. In listening, we discover our gifting, and in obedience, we gain wisdom. There is so much more as we walk together with the Father and each other.

Come and go with me. There is joy, joy, joy!

THE CALL

1

THE CALL

Just as the calling of Abraham differed from the call of Samuel, so God speaks uniquely to each of us. Some may have a dramatic sense of calling while others receive a gentle nudge to experience God in a new season of growth. My own calling came as a surprise in a tiny African village, while Cookie's resulted from powerful images that jolted her expectations.

How is God calling you?

HELLO, GOLI

"For I know the plans I have for you," declares the
Lord, "plans to prosper you and not to harm you,
plans to give you hope and a future"
— Jeremiah 29:11 (NIV)

I wasn't even asking for direction when God showed up at my
door in the form of my friend Helen. "Marthe, the bishop has a
conflict for our upcoming trip to Uganda, and he'd like to know if
you can go."

Without pausing for breath or asking my permission, my mother,
who was visiting, said, "She can go." Just like that. And that's how
I made my first diocesan mission trip.

After a rich and happy season of marriage, my husband had
just passed away. My mom, pastor, and I had completed plans for
celebration of his life, and I had only one specific request: "I want
my friend Debbie to sing 'I Know That My Redeemer Liveth,' from
Messiah. It's a beautiful statement of faith, and Peter would have
loved it." And with that, my journey took another turn.

Goli, our mission base, is a beautiful little village stuck in a
remote corner of northwestern Uganda. One does not accidentally
arrive at Goli. It is too far off the beaten path.

Electricity had not yet reached this remote outpost, nor had
indoor plumbing. Most of the floors were dirt, and the houses
sported beautifully thatched roofs. Community buildings were
sparse and made of cinder block with concrete floors. And yes, the
people of Goli were some of the richest people I had ever met—rich
in love, faith, and good deeds.

Our small team traveled throughout the leafy-green district for
three weeks hearing schoolchildren recite memory verses, speaking

at countless village churches, conducting Bible studies, visiting women's groups, meeting local missionaries, and making friends. The Sunday before we left was Easter. It was not lost on me that my first Easter without Peter found me on the mission field among scores of new friends who love Jesus just as we do.

After the service at the village cathedral, Sister Kim, the Korean missionary, invited us to brunch at her house. We stood in a circle around the table, holding hands for the blessing. As we finished, Sister Kim reached over to a shelf and pushed the button on a battery-powered tape recorder. Out of that small piece of technology rolled the words, "I know that my redeemer liveth."

Coincidence? Immediately, I sensed that God had a plan to give a newly minted widow a future and a hope. One era had ended; a new one in Christ had begun.

Reflection

Do we really want to hear from God? What might he say that would challenge our status quo or show us that there's so much more beyond our finite purview? Does fear hinder us from giving ourselves unreservedly to God for his use, in his time, in his way?

What would you like to see God do in your life?

_____

_____

_____

_____

What hinders you from complete embrace of God's direction and his plan?

_____

_____

_____

_____

What steps can you take to learn more about your call?

_____

_____

_____

_____

Sweet Lord, you do walk with us through the valley of the shadow to take us to the other side. And your plans far surpass our wildest dreams. Thank you. Amen.

WHAT DO I HAVE?

Then the Lord said to him, What is that in your
hand? "A staff," he replied. The Lord said, "Throw
it on the ground."

—Exodus 4:2–3 (NIV)

Although reluctantly, Eric agreed to go on his first mission to
Africa to be part of a women's conference. After committing to
the trip, Eric spent time wondering what he had that he could give
and do for *a women's conference in Uganda.* As circumstances proved,
Eric had a pocketful of seeds for the future. The team leader had a
prolonged recovery from a planned surgery, and Eric was promoted
from team member to team leader.

After arriving in Kampala, the capital, Eric and the team
established themselves in the church guesthouse. Eric walked up
the hill to the cathedral where he encountered a young man playing
a trumpet. Since Eric also played trumpet, the two found a used
trumpet in the practice room, and Namirembe Hill resonated for a
couple of hours with soulful trumpet duets.

The team moved on to the next place of ministry, where Eric
discovered that the English brass band tradition was alive there
as well as all over the country. In another place scheduled for a
stopover, band members emerged, and Eric was hooked. (The
women's conference was conducted to the joy of all participants, but
it appeared that Eric's calling was to something entirely different.)

Upon returning to the states, Eric told his story to other musician
friends, and the beginning of a vital ministry to young people was
launched. The following year the newly constituted Band & Bible
Mission met with bands in the three locations Eric had visited. Team

members taught music, instrument repair, Bible, and practical life skills.

As the mission has grown, scholarships and tutoring (done by band members) have been added, and members are becoming self-sustaining. All because Eric said *yes* to joining a team conducting a women's conference.

Reflection

Isn't it amazing how God directs our hearts as well as our minds while he quietly molds and conforms us to do his will? Like Abraham, who set out not knowing where he was going (Hebrews 11:8), we obediently go, at times hesitantly, but trusting God all the while. And the richness and joy of the journey is beyond anything we could think or imagine.

I think of Mother Theresa, who chose to leave a comfortable convent to work among the poorest of the poor in the slums of Calcutta. There was George Mueller, who pioneered orphanages for more than ten thousand orphans in Bristol when this was not yet popular with society. John Newton, slave trader and investor, became a fierce abolitionist after his conversion. And Sadhu Sundar Singh, "the apostle with the bleeding feet"[1] in India, touched lives with his gentle, loving ministry to human and beast. What might God do with us?

What dream has God given you that you long to achieve?

_____

_____

_____

Write a prayer of trust and petition that you might become all God desires for you.

_____

_____

_____

Father, we rarely know our destination when we begin to follow you. Give us courage and anticipation to boldly step out of our comfortable spaces to be your disciples. In Jesus's name. Amen.

FOLLOWING THE CALL

Let us run with perseverance the race marked out
for us, fixing our eyes on Jesus.

—Hebrews 12:1–2 (NIV)

I met John in Honduras. He was a carpenter by trade and was invited to go to Honduras with a mission team. John was so moved by what he saw and experienced that he gladly returned. And then he went again. Finally, on his fourth mission, Helen, his wife, joined him. Helen and John found themselves so strangely touched by the people and work that soon nothing felt foreign.

When the middle-aged couple returned home, they began praying and asking for God's direction. Two of their four children were married, and the other two were at university. John and Helen felt called to leave everything and give their lives to minister in the mountains of Honduras.

I asked Helen if it was terribly hard for her to leave her children and home to serve in a country thousands of miles away. Her eyes misted, and she nodded. She said that at first, the two youngest children were angry, even though they were well situated at school. Nevertheless, she and John knew they had to follow where God was leading them.

They began working in a medical clinic with logistics and administration, all the while filling their days with prayer and trust. Through difficult times John said God continued to challenge him with, "Can you trust me?" They stayed the course, relying fully on God's provision, grace, and guidance.

Today, their children, all grown, visit, affirming the ministry and their parents' call. They tell Helen and John how proud they are of them, for they now understand and have their own personal walks with the Lord. The clinic has grown and has sixteen staff members including doctors, medical specialists, and technologists. Thousands of mountain people are served every year, and many come to know Jesus.

Because two people decided to give themselves to follow Jesus.

Reflection

A friend told me that as a young person, she thought that if she refused to learn Swahili, she wouldn't have to go to Africa. She voiced what I've heard others say who fear the cost of following Jesus.

I wonder if we would find our fears slipping away if we immersed ourselves in the expressions of Jesus's love—the feeding of the hungry (thousands at a time), healing of the sick, forgiveness of sinners, loving the marginalized, and so much more. Can we replace fear with faith as we contemplate and grow in love for the one who loved us first?

Have you ever wondered what God would do *to* you (rather than *in* you) if you said, "Yes," without reservation?

_____

_____

_____

_____

_____

What words of assurance have you heard or read that encourage you to follow on?

_____

_____

_____

_____

_____

Father, open our ears so that we may hear when you call, and give us courage to trust your leading. In Jesus's name. Amen.

COOKIE'S CALL

[He] is able to do exceedingly abundantly above all
that we ask or think, according to the power that
works in us.
　　—Ephesians 3:20–21 (New King James Version)

Cookie has come home to renew her visa. She returns from Haiti every few months so she can go back to work with orphans in their hillside sanctuary. Two years ago, she responded to God's call to go—just for a few months—and now she finds herself returning again and again.

Cookie teaches English and is committed to helping every one of her students learn to communicate in English. She knows that speaking English in Haiti is almost a sure guarantee of a decent job in the stressed economy. But that's not why Cookie continues to return to Haiti after every break. She told us about one of the many ways she sees God at work.

A young mother came to the orphanage to confess that she had thrown her newborn into a garbage dump—about twelve hours earlier. Cookie and her colleagues had become inured to finding little ones who were discarded for one reason or another, but it was unusual for a mother to come bearing the news.

The group rushed to a large trough, sixteen feet deep, where the baby had been tossed earlier in the day. One of the young men climbed into the pit, rummaged around, and found a plastic bag containing the baby. He hauled it up and put it on the ground as the others gathered round to pray. An inert little arm fell out of the bag, and as they prayed, they heard the sound of a gasping intake of breath and then a cry. Miraculously, the baby girl was alive, unscratched, unmarked.

The missioners brought the little bundle back to their compound and cleaned her up, all the while thanking God for sparing her. One of the missionary couples reached out to adopt the baby, naming her Faith, and she is now a thriving toddler who is loved and coddled by all the missioners on campus.

And so, Cookie keeps going back to Haiti.*

*Due to the extreme violence and kidnappings in Haiti, mission work has been put on hold. This was written in a more peaceful time, and the Good News it shares is still relevant.

Reflection

It is easy to be intimidated when we hear of someone else's personal experience with calling: "That's never happened to me," or "I could never do that." We get ourselves into comparison games and usually fall short.

But God doesn't call us to walk someone else's path nor follow someone else's call. Each of us with our own distinct genetic makeup created by a God who crafted our life plan has a personally designed ministry to which we are perfectly suited.

What gifts have you or others discovered in your life?

_____

_____

How might you hone those skills for God's use?

_____

_____

Father, thank you that, just like each distinct snowflake, we are unique and exquisitely created by you. Strengthen our faith to receive your calling designed just for us. In Jesus our Lord. Amen.

PRODUCT OF THE CHURCH

Train up a child in the way he should go: and when
he is old, he will not depart from it.
                    —Proverbs 22:6 (King James Version)

A s Jim tells it, he got acquainted with Sunday school through
a neighbor lady on his block. Every Sunday, she did what
[Christian] neighbor ladies with cars do best on Sunday mornings—
she gathered all the children, and they made their way to Sunday
school. It would have stayed that way, he said, until the preacher
started yelling at him. He always seemed to be angry about
something, so Jim left.

When he was an adolescent, Jim's mom discovered an Episcopal
church with a "missionary zeal." She took Jim with her, and he was
hooked. He became an acolyte, sang in the junior choir, and was
eventually a church lay-leader. To his wonder and delight, someone
gave him a free ride to Trinity University. (Jim was one of seven
students in his high school graduating class to go on to college.)

Seeing his "love affair with the church" and its Lord, the
diocesan bishop asked him one day if he'd ever thought of going
to seminary. He concluded with, "The church needs you." And that
was just the beginning of Jim's call. Seminary years passed quickly,
and then came a string of church assignments—Jim's bishop was
impatient with clergy who only served one congregation at a time.

Traversing from one congregation to another, Jim's love for
mission and healthy stewardship grew. Arriving at a parish in
northwest Texas, he cast a vision challenging the church to embrace
a program of, what he called, fifty-fifty giving. For every dollar
that was received, fifty cents would be given to mission. Within
two years, the parish budget increased from $120,000 to more

than $800,000 per year. And through their missionary outreach, extraordinary things occurred.

One Sunday in 1984, Jim stood at the church door and gave every person a five dollar bill to use for mission and to bring the return back in four months. A widow started a business and brought "a good return" back to the church. A family held a fellowship dinner in the parish hall and doubled their money, which went back to the church for ministry. A rancher filled sacks with cow manure and sold them for a profit three times the cost. At the end of the experiment, the church had $42,000 to be used for mission.

Under Jim's leadership, his parishioners were involved in ministry in a hospital in Israel and helped resettle more than seven hundred refugees. As his diocese recognized God's call on his life, he was elected bishop. One of the first things he did in his office was to establish a Department of World Missions, charging it with responsibility to call the diocese to reconnect with our precious history as a missionary people.

Jim likes to say that he is a product of the church. I think it would be apropos to add that he is also a product of two women determined to help him find his faith and his own determination to discover and pursue God for himself.

Reflection

Most churches provide opportunities for spiritual education (e.g., Sunday school, confirmation) and fellowship. What part do you see the Christian family has in shaping their children's knowledge of God and spiritual things?

_____

_____

List some of the parents mentioned in Scripture along with their influence on their children:

_____

_____

Write a prayer for the spiritual growth and nurturing of your children:

_____

_____

_____

BEING THE TWELFTH MAN

Then I heard the voice of the Lord saying, "Whom shall I send? And who will go for us?" And I said, "Here am I. Send me!"

—Isaiah 6:8 (NIV)

With two granddaughters at Texas A&M University, I've observed that the student body stands throughout the whole of every football game. Our missioner Karen said that this practice goes way back to 1922 when A&M was playing in the first bowl game of the Southwest Conference against the nation's top-rated team. Coach Dana X. Bible watched helplessly as injuries piled up, depleting his reserves.

As the game neared halftime, Coach Bible remembered a player who had not made the traveling team but who told the coach, "I'll be in the stands if you need me."

The coach sent a messenger to find the young player to suit up for the second half. The young man stood on the sidelines throughout the rest of the game that A&M won and was the only man left standing on the sidelines for the Aggies. He later said, "I wish I could say that I went in and ran for the winning touchdown, but I did not. I simply stood by in case my team needed me."

This is how the Texas A&M tradition of the twelfth man began and why students stand ready to be called on to the field.

Having been called to work with our water mission, Karen thinks our role is to be that "twelfth man" whether or not we think we have the proper skills or training. What God is really looking for is a willing spirit, ready to serve when he asks, "Whom shall I send?"

Karen says she and her husband, Don (a former A&M professor), haven't spent years going on missions because they like beans and love to sweat. They go because they feel God has called them out of the stands to be his hands and feet and to serve as his twelfth man.

"Here I am. Send me."

Reflection

Availability and willingness seem to be key factors in being that twelfth man. When we examine the stories of the original disciples, it becomes obvious that perfection or piety or humility are not required to answer God's call. Being present, saying yes, and allowing God to put us in the place of his choice is what he desires.

If you were writing a job description for being God's twelfth man, what would you say?

_____

_____

_____

Are you ready to fill in a gap no matter the difficulties?

_____

_____

_____

Father, help us to be ready to go whenever and wherever you need us. Thank you. Amen.

TAPESTRIES

Each of you should use whatever gift you have
received to serve others, as faithful stewards of
God's grace in its various forms.

—1 Peter 4:10 (NIV)

Some years ago, Brenda, an internationally recognized artist, wanted to participate in missions but questioned what she had to give. She wondered if God could possibly have a special assignment for her. And then she was invited to go to Honduras. A simple invitation encouraged her to offer her gifts for God's use and shaped the trajectory of her calling.

Brenda discovered that her patient instruction gently stirred the creative gifts that lay dormant in the hearts and hands of the precious women she encountered. She taught about color, design, form, and texture and watched the ladies begin to fashion their own masterpieces with needle and thread and bits of fabric. And as they worked, their relationships strengthened and their confidence soared.

After a few joyful weeks with her first class, Brenda gathered the beautiful tapestries to take to market for her students. With the proceeds from their initial offerings, the women discovered that they could pay school fees for their children and buy many other household necessities. Perhaps the greatest benefit arising from Brenda's presence was not the development of a microenterprise but that the women had come together in community loving and supporting one another.

In a later iteration and location of the ministry, women have written a constitution declaring their new identity and their new self-confidence. They have elected officers and have expanded their meetings to include Bible studies, singing, dancing, and public health.

Brenda's calling had begun by asking God what she had to give to mission work, and God responded with a group of vibrant souls whose lives were transformed through her desire to give. She would go on to work with others in her parish, and Helen would join her in developing a business, Threads of Blessing, that would touch even more lives in other countries.

Reflection

I read about a man who, after learning of the contributions of other Christians, became so discouraged with his own life that he sank into despair. It's easy enough to be blinded to our own particularities that we fail to grasp the needs and opportunities that only we can fulfill.

There's a wonderful story about Gideon (Judges 6:1–7, 25), who is called to deliver Israel from their enemies. He doubts his ability to lead, but God gently calms his fears and forms him into exactly what is needed. What seems to deter you from allowing God to use you for his service?

_____

_____

Who or what encourages you to step out in faith to places you've never gone?

_____

_____

_____

How can you begin to trust God's leading for your life?

_____

_____

Father, make us bold to examine those niggling questions that so often lead us straight to you. Amen.

PAINTING THE CROSS

Before I formed you in the womb I knew you, and before you were born I consecrated you.
—Jeremiah 1:5 (English Standard Version)

For generations, youth meetings have been fertile soil for our young people as they come together to hear God's voice and grow in their faith. And it was so with one of my dear clergy friends.

When Justin was twelve years old, he attended a youth gathering in the Southern California region where he was living. His youth group stayed in the conference hotel and had a great time.

The gathering was for three days, and on Saturday evening Justin was sitting in the ballroom with five hundred other youth listening to the energetic speaker. She spoke about spiritual gifts and God's calling to each one of them for a certain purpose. He was mesmerized. Every word she said meant something. He sat on the floor, but he said if he had been in a chair, he would have been on the edge of his seat.

The speaker asked adults to hand out big sheets of paper along with a wide range of art supplies. She invited all her young audience to draw, paint, color, or even write how God was calling them. My friend sat there in awe, overwhelmed with a sense of call to ordained ministry.

Carefully and with purposeful intent, he took brown paint and, using his thumb as a brush, finger-painted a cross. Next, he took red paint and put three swipes of red with his finger for the blood of Christ coming off the cross.

Justin began to weep. His youth minister came to see if he was all right. Immediately, he proclaimed that God had called him to be a minister. Jim, the youth minister, mentored him over the years before college, and when he graduated, Justin entered seminary. Since finishing seminary, Justin has served as a priest in the church.

When he was ordained, a copy of the finger-painted picture was printed in his ordination bulletin, and to this day, that framed picture hangs on the wall in Justin's office as a reminder of the reality of God's call.

Reflection

Justin is not the only person I know who heard God's voice at a young age. I think of Edith who "gave her heart to Jesus" as a five-year-old and went on to be a church musician and mentor. Bill responded to God's call when his Sunday school teacher told him about Jesus and is a marvelous consultant for youth camps. And there are so many others.

Do we ever discount the capacity of children to grasp God's immeasurable, unconditional love? Even the disciples failed to appreciate the attraction that drew children to Jesus. They were ready to push the young ones aside. But Jesus ...

Do you recall a time when, as a child, God called you to do something for him?

_____

_____

Did you or have you acted on that call?

_____

_____

How can you "bring the little ones" to Jesus?

_____

_____

Have you considered teaching a children's Sunday school class or helping with youth activities? Mentoring? Big Brother?

_____

_____

Father, thank you for not looking at age or size. Help us to see hearts and use us as encouragers, especially for all your precious little ones. In Jesus's name. Amen.

"I HAVE NEVER FORGOTTEN"

Use your head—and heart!—to discern what is
right, to test what is authentically right.
—John 7:24 (The Message)

E dwina has been involved in world missions for the last thirty-
five years and served nineteen years as national director of an
international missions organization. I asked Edwina about her
calling, and this was her response.

"As a young teen I was part of a 'pack' of sweaty, giggly friends
who were at a church camp for girls located deep in the piney woods
of East Texas. We jammed into the back of a large gathering hall to
listen to two women give a 'chalk talk.' One of the missionaries told
the story, and the other used colored chalk to bring the picture to
life. I was enthralled by both. That night my heart began to pound
hard when the invitation was spoken to 'give your life for full-time
Christian service.' I said yes and walked to the front.

"We went outside to a shelter covering a picnic table and lighted
by a single hanging lightbulb. Looking around, I realized with
something like panic that all the others who responded to that
particular call were camp counselors. I received a card to fill out:
name, phone number, church, pastor ...

"My pastor called my mother, and she drove me to the church
for my appointment—the first time I had been in the pastor's office,
and probably the first time I had had a one-on-one conversation with
him. The entire conversation has long been erased, except for his last
words: 'You are too young to make this decision.'

"And I was too young: In my immaturity, I internally processed
this as, 'God doesn't want me. I tried. Made a mistake.' So life

happened. College. Marriage. Motherhood. Housewife. And growing in discipleship.

"At age forty-three I was invited on my first short-term mission trip to Kenya and Uganda. I applied for a passport for the first international trip of my life. After a stop in London for team building, we flew to Nairobi. I was sitting by the plane's window, awed by the sight of the Alps with their fresh November snow and deep shadows cast by the bright sunshine. My spirit began to soar with praise.

"In that intimate moment, I had a flashback to the gathering around the picnic table, and I heard his clear voice in my mind: 'You may have forgotten, but I have never forgotten.'"

Reflection

In the dark of the night, young Samuel heard a voice that he thought was Eli, the priest. We don't know what time it was, but Samuel was quick to respond. And Eli was quick to send him back to bed. This happened several times, and each time Samuel rushed to Eli's side. Eli gifted the whole of Israel (and us) when, in his prophetic insight, he recognized God's intervention in the child's life.

Just as with Samuel, did you ever sense God's calling you as a child?

_____

_____

How did you respond?

_____

_____

If you overlooked that call as you grew older, might this be a time to recapture that moment when God was speaking to your heart in a particular way and for a particular service?

_____

_____

If you are remembering a distant call from God, how will you respond?

_____

_____

Father, thank you that your reach touches all of us. Help us to be sensitive to your voice and to pay special attention to the little ones whose hearing is often more attuned than ours. In Jesus's name. Amen.

FOR SUCH A TIME AS THIS

> And who knows whether you have not come to the
> kingdom for such a time as this?
>   —Esther 4:14 (ESV)

The Bible is replete with stories of ordinary people doing extraordinary things. Esther, an orphan who was raised by her uncle, became the person through whom God rescued his people from certain death. Young David learned courage keeping his sheep and fearlessly rescued the Israelites from destruction. Peter and his brother, Andrew, were fishermen who joined a motley crew to become Jesus's trusted disciples. God uses the willing among us.

Retiring monk Telemachus[2] felt called to go to Rome without any clear indication of what he would do once he arrived. Upon hearing the roar of the crowds when he neared the Coliseum, he ventured closer to learn that people were being sacrificed to wild animals for entertainment.

It is said that the godly man pushed his way through the barriers until he stood in the middle of the arena. "Desist, desist," he shouted. This unexpected happening stunned the crowd to silence, and then they began to call for his blood, even as he continued to shout for an end to the violence. As he was being stoned, he did not know that his death would bring about the end of the gladiatorial games.

We have visionaries on our own soil who pledged lives and resources for the ideal of religious freedom. In other places, Wilberforce dedicated his life and energies to abolishing slavery in Britain, while Bonhoeffer's passion for living out the Gospel led him to perish attempting to destroy the evil that corrupted his beloved German homeland. The list goes on.

History reminds us that God's people always have a responsibility to understand the times and to respond in obedience to his providence. *To what has God called you for such a time as this?*

Reflection

Have you thought of what you might have accomplished with a degree? Or if your childhood hadn't been so chaotic? Or if your circumstances had been different? Do you ever wish you could have "do-overs"? There are videos and books written about these topics, but for people of faith, especially followers of Jesus, we believe that God takes all the disparate pieces of our lives and makes something really good. He uses our *ordinariness* combined with our submitted hearts to bring about his kingdom.

How many of us had ever heard of Telemachus? Yet God used his compassion to end the cruelty of Rome's bloody gladiatorial games.

Is something stirring in your heart, a circumstance where your voice might make a difference?

_____

_____

How can you prepare yourself to be God's instrument?

_____

_____

God's Word can direct us in our efforts to do his will. Memorize 1 Corinthians 1:27 "But God chose the foolish things of the world to shame the wise; God chose the weak things of the world to shame the strong" (NIV).

Father, each of us has a role in your providential plan. Open our eyes to see how we may faithfully serve you and the community in which you have placed us. In Jesus's name. Amen.

MEASURING UP

Teach me thy way, O Lord; I will walk in thy truth:
unite my heart to fear thy name.
                                     —Psalm 86:11 (KJV)

M issionary Elisabeth Elliot mentions in her book *Keep a
Quiet Heart*[3] that she attended boarding school where the
headmistress required students to keep the Asian rugs (and the
fringe) straight. I look around at the rugs on my floors that have
corners nibbled by decades of puppies and fringes worn down to
the warp. If Ms. Elliot had ever come to visit, I would have had to
remove the rugs so I could measure up.

Or not? God didn't call me to be Elisabeth Elliot or Mother
Theresa or Ruth Graham or Julian of Norwich. And he didn't call
them to do the things that are part of my calling. I would love to think
that being part of a caring household drew the foster children, extra
cousins, and children of friends who made their home with us. Even
if I'd wanted to, I couldn't prioritize the rugs—instead, the additional
people warmed the house and added vitality and interest. (We did
have a couple of grandchildren live with us, and, to my astonishment,
without any coaching, one actually went around straightening fringes.)

What God calls one saint to do may not be the calling of another.
We all have our gifts that he uses, and they are individually tailored.
We can't allow ourselves to be intimidated because our rugs are out
of order, our sermons don't measure up to Phillips Brooks's, or we
cannot pray like Paul. We didn't choose God; he chose us (John
15:16 NIV) because he saw something distinctive in us that was in
none of his other children.

It's time we go forth rejoicing in him and the glorious doors of
opportunity he opens *in the going.* Yes, Lord, yes.

Reflection

Can you think of people in the Bible who didn't seem qualified for the assignment God placed with them? Moses is an obvious candidate. Remember, he told God that he couldn't speak (much less lead). Samson had a weakness for women, and God used him to deliver the Israelites numbers of times. Amos tended fig trees, but God made him a prophet.

In the list of people we might not have chosen in the holy entourage, we should include Rahab, a prostitute who was the great-great-grandmother of King David. Ruth, a Moabitess (whose people were idolaters) and Bathsheba (assaulted by King David) were also ancestors of Jesus. God, whose ways are far beyond ours, looks for someone whose heart is turned toward and open to him.

How would you describe God followers?

_____

_____

Do you see yourself in that crowd?_____

Why or why not?_____

_____

Early Christians were called people of the Way. They hadn't yet arrived, but they were "on the way."

Father, open our ears to your voice, and give us a heart of faith and trust. Keep us from the temptation of measuring ourselves by others. Instead, you be our measuring stick. Let your approval be our reward, and lead us in your way. In Jesus's name. Amen.

EMBRACING THE CALL

Each person should live as a believer in whatever situation the Lord has assigned to them, just as God has called them.

—1 Corinthians 7:17 (NIV)

O ften, God's call emerges from a profession or life work in which we're already engaged. I know a number of clergy and lay leaders who began ministry as camp counselors; others began in a variety of occupations. Some of the most inspirational leaders I know minister from their homes. All it takes is a heart open to his leading.

Jeanne Guyon[4] was the daughter of wealthy parents in seventeenth-century France. When she reached her fifteenth birthday, she was forced into a loveless marriage with a much older man. Her mother-in-law and maid regularly abused her, and she suffered the deaths of three of her children before finally being widowed.

All the while disappointments would seem to crush her, Mme. Guyon early on chose to listen to God's voice within. The religious world of her time was reeling with disunity, but Jeanne Guyon quietly surrendered her life to be used as God desired. Mme. Guyon renounced all personal possessions and expended her wealth in outreach to other seekers.

History records that Guyon's family intensified their persecution, and she was eventually imprisoned for her faith. In prison, she was nightly visited by hungry souls who came to her cell window for counsel and spiritual direction. Though often exhausted, she never failed to share her simple gifts of God's love and grace.

Faithful even in the middle of extreme suffering, Jeanne Guyon employed her life circumstances as the venue for her vocation.

Guyon's writings still live on as testaments to a life of joy and intimacy with her Father, who brought healing and redemption as she journeyed with him. She chose to use her suffering to bring life and healing. So can we.

Reflection

Name the people in your life who have inspired and encouraged you in your Christian journey.

_____

_____

Are any of them what we call laypeople?

_____

_____

What unique gifts do you possess that could be used to strengthen others?

_____

_____

Father, thank you for making a space for all of us to work and share in your glorious kingdom. In Jesus our Lord. Amen.

GOING

Everyone who calls on the name of the Lord will be saved. How, then, can they call on the one they have not believed in? And how can they believe in the one of whom they have not heard? And how can they hear without someone preaching to them?
—Romans 10:13–14 (NIV)

D id you know that in the old days, when people heard the call to become a missionary, it typically meant leaving home, family, and all comforts for a lifetime? And global travel was a matter of months rather than hours crossing one continent to another.

Missionaries of another time packed their worldly belongings in wooden coffins, knowing that when they returned home it would be in that box. Following God's call to preach the Gospel to those who have not yet heard was a costly commitment, but those pioneer missionaries whose hearts were afire with God's love were determined to share God's Good News with the unreached.

The stirring book *Heroines of Missionary Adventure*[5] is filled with stories of young women who heard the call to go, determined to leave all to share God's love to natives in India, Egypt, Africa, Greenland, China, and other places. One of the characteristics that predominates in these tales of courage and sacrifice is the warmth of Christ's love in reaching out to those who did not yet know him.

Mary Louisa Whately of Dublin went to Cairo looking for a warmer winter climate. Together with a cousin, she rented a house in a poor neighborhood, hoping to open a school. The women went door to door inviting mothers to send their daughters to their home to learn, and on the following day they taught Bible stories, the alphabet, singing, and sewing. The school grew and continued until Mary was recalled home to Ireland.

After a while, she returned to Cairo with her maid, and her students enthusiastically returned. As the students and staff grew, Mary became skilled at treating eye diseases, and she began doing missionary work along the Nile. Mary's teaching and life were so authentic as to create strong disciples among her students. Even during times of great hardship, they stood firm in their faith.

As she approached her sixty-sixth year, Mary was ministering on the Nile. She had caught a cold but refused to stop her work because the people were expecting her. Not until she visited the last village on her route would she return to Cairo.

Long after her passing, her faithful love for her Lord and the people of Egypt would leave a lasting legacy. While Mary left her homeland with no intention of becoming a missionary, her heart of love and sensitivity to her neighbors spoke to the gifts that God had already placed in her. In the same way, God will plant us where there is need and open our eyes to how he can work and love and touch through us.

Reflection

On All Saints' Day, many churches sing the favorite hymn, "I Sing A Song of the Saints of God":

> I sing a song of the saints of God,
> Patient and brave and true,
> Who toiled and fought and lived and died
> For the Lord they loved and knew.
> And one was a doctor, and one was a queen,
> And one was a shepherdess on the green:
> They were all of them saints of God, and I mean,
> God helping, to be one too.
> (Lesbia Scott, 1929)

One of the many things I love about this song is that it indicates saints who are doctors, queens, shepherdesses, and in another stanza, we find soldiers and priests. In other words, saints (holy or virtuous people) are everywhere. God finds them wherever they are and places them wherever he sees the need.

You have been strategically placed by God for ministry. Pray, asking God to show you how you might glorify him right where you are.

Father, remind us that when we follow you, we rely on your strength and love in us and not on ourselves. Thank you. Amen.

FROM ECUADOR

For whoever wants to save their life will lose it, but
whoever loses their life for me will find it.
—Matthew 16:25 (NIV)

He had come back for the funeral. Rachel Saint, his aunt, was
a missionary to the Waodani Indians (the Waos) and died
after living with them for thirty-six years. Steve had lived with the
Waodani as a child but returned to the states to attend college. And
then Rachel passed away.

You may be familiar with the story. Steve's father, Nate Saint,
was a pilot for Missionary Aviation Fellowship (MAF) and had been
among five missionaries who devised a plan to make contact with
the Waodani, a fierce tribe known for violence and revenge killings.

For several months, Saint flew over Waodani encampments
dropping gifts, which were soon reciprocated. The missionary spoke
words of friendship and peace through a loudspeaker. Before long,
Saint and his friends deemed the Waodani open to their efforts
at communication, and they staged a meeting point on a sandy
riverbank.

As hoped, several Waodani approached the missionaries;
however, two left without explanation, carrying false reports back
to their tribesmen. The missionaries awaited the return of the group
but were soon attacked, and each one was slaughtered. The Waodani
escaped into the jungle. A massive search party discovered four of
the bodies—it was assumed the other had washed away—and they
were buried in a common grave.

The following year, Nate Saint's sister Rachel and another
missionary widow, Elisabeth Elliot, and her daughter, returned to
Ecuador to live near and minister to the Waodani. Their efforts

eventually brought peace among warring tribes and economic development, and many natives, including Mincaye, the man who had killed Steve's father, became Christians. A bond grew between the two, and Mincaye took a special responsibility for raising Steve. He adopted Steve as his tribal son. In time, Elisabeth and her daughter returned to the states, but Rachel stayed on until her death.

At Rachel's funeral, the community that had killed his father asked Steve Saint if he and his family would come live and work among them. After prayer and discussion, the Saints moved to Ecuador, where Steve[6] helped the tribe achieve economic growth and self-determination. And many more of the Waodani came to know Jesus.

Reflection

In the Lord's Prayer (Matthew 6:9–13), Jesus speaks specifically about forgiveness. What instructions does he give us?

_____

_____

Is forgiveness a discipline, a decision, or both?

_____

_____

Explain:

_____

_____

What inhibits us from forgiving?

_____

_____

Name some benefits of forgiving:

_____

_____

As you call us to forgive, Father, remind us what it cost Jesus to forgive us. Amen.

LED

I being in the way, the Lord led me.
—Genesis 24:27 (KJV)

In trying to find a common denominator that draws people to ministry or to a specific work, I've interviewed numerous people. Father John worked for years with street people, people with addictions, and otherwise marginalized souls. When he was invited to join other clergy on a Native American reservation, John knew he was ready and had been prepared.

Kurt and Ellen, a married clergy couple with five special-needs children, sensed they had completed their present assignment, and it was time to move on. When the invitation came, they accepted a call to mission work.

Mercy, whose priest father told her, "You'd be a good priest," was primed for God's call and knew "that was where [she] was supposed to be." Jonathan also grew up in a clergyman's home, had become a priest and received a note at a retreat confirming what God was already doing in his heart. He said *yes* to the call.

Long ago, there was Eliezer, Abraham's trusted servant (Genesis 24). Abraham sent Eliezer to get a bride for his son of promise, Isaac. In obedience, Eliezer set off from camp heading to Nahor, a journey of hundreds of miles. When he reached the outskirts of the town, he prayed for guidance.

Beautiful Rebecca appeared "before he had finished praying" (Genesis 24:15). Rebecca gave Eliezer water, watered his twelve camels—a feat in itself—and then took him home to meet her family. The servant didn't seem at all surprised to learn that Rebecca was related to Abraham and eligible to marry his master's son. In fact, he confidently admitted that putting himself on the path to obedience was where he found God's leadership.

It is comforting to learn that all God asks is that we be willing, pliable, and ready to do his will. He qualifies those he calls, and the common denominator seems to be a readiness to be willing. God supplies the call and the direction. He gives us the tools and training and manages the logistics.

Reflection

I have read that there are sound waves that cause air particles to vibrate and collide with each other, passing the sound through our ears and to the eardrum. This is how we hear. If that's a natural phenomenon, it seems only reasonable that God would be able to communicate with us in ways we can't observe but are, nevertheless, real. In fact, I believe God is speaking all the time, but we aren't always "tuned in."

Jesus said his sheep know his voice and follow him (John 10:27), and he wouldn't say something that isn't true. Could it be that we need to practice listening and becoming familiar with the voice of our Savior?

Have you ever had a hearing test where numerous sounds come at different frequencies and tones? At first it's difficult to determine if the sound is real or if it's a figment of an eager imagination. One must focus to respond to the beeps.

And an expectation that he will speak, even to us, prepares us to listen. Time to practice.

What would you like God to say to you?

_____

_____

How can you prepare to hear his voice?

_____

_____

What are some scripture verses that encourage us to listen?

_____

_____

Father, Jesus said that his sheep know his voice. Help us to recognize his voice and yours when you speak. In his name we pray. Amen.

GETTING READY

2

GETTING READY

Travel nowadays is not for the faint-hearted, from coordinating schedules, editing a wardrobe, and learning about another culture to conforming to differing expectations. In a similar fashion, our faith journey needs preparation. We learn from our guidebook and those who are seasoned travelers, we determine the cost as well as the value of the journey, and we begin to practice the disciplines that will ensure safe passage. What are you doing to get ready?

WHY NOT START
WITH PRAYER?

As for me, far be it from me that I should sin against
the Lord by failing to pray for you.
—1 Samuel 12:23 (NIV)

During the Enlightenment, the *philosophes* and many religious
leaders embraced the superiority of classical philosophy in
contrast to Christian faith and ideas. What a disillusionment it
must have been to see the human and moral failure of the French
Revolution and intellect—even though initially infused with high
ideals.

And then the romanticists turned to feelings to liberate the
human spirit. The imagination was freed to soar to God, to turn to
him to touch man's deepest needs. But feelings, too, were insufficient
to bring us into a satisfying, consistent relationship with the divine.

The Marxists propagated the notion that religion is a creation
of the people and their response to social and economic conditions.
Essentially, addressing economic and social ills would, in time,
eliminate spiritual hunger.

And so on.

Given my own spiritual responsibilities, I attended a religious
conference designed to explore issues in the church. Guest speakers
(recognized experts in their fields) dissected the concerns from every
imaginable position but suggested no cogent plan or resolution.
During the break, I was so frustrated, I approached a couple of
the "experts" and suggested that these were the same issues with
the same arguments that we'd heard at the last conference. Had
it occurred to anyone that, since we don't seem to have answers,

perhaps we might gather to pray? To seek divine guidance? To ask God for healing and wisdom?

There was dead silence until one of the clergy standing nearby said, "You can use my church."

I find it easy to speak when I should be listening—for the voice that directs me to love, to heal, to lift, to encourage rather than be distracted by the problem. Like Peter when he looked at the waves rather than Jesus, sinking is inevitable. Praying and listening can be done collectively or solo, and they always prepare us for ministry.

"God forbid that I should sin ... in ceasing to pray for you" (1 Samuel 12:23 KJV). It's a start.

Reflection

I've been part of a number of Bible studies and various religious groups throughout the years. I've participated in committees focused on spiritual renewal. All in all, it seems that we (myself included) are so much more comfortable exploring, studying, and discussing issues than we are praying together about them. The most we can ever hope to get out of our meetings is informed opinions but no real power to affect the change that is needed.

Several years ago, our church asked parishioners to volunteer to pray for one hour daily through the season of Pentecost. To hold us accountable, they asked that we affix our names to the signup sheet that would be published. After some debate, I signed up along with others and found it to be one of the single most growth-inspiring disciplines I'd ever discovered. When the period of prayer was ended, I found I didn't want to stop. I had tiptoed into what Brother Lawrence might have called *the practice of the presence of God.*[7]

Prior to teaching about prayer, Jesus said to his disciples, "When you pray" (Matthew 6:5–7 NIV), not *if* you pray. Are you satisfied with your prayer discipline?

_____

_____

If not, what would you like to see change?

_____

_____

Do a Google search on scripture verses about prayer. List some of your favorites:

_____

_____

Read a biography on someone known as a person of prayer (for example, Brother Lawrence, George Mueller, John Hyde, John Wesley). Note the effects on his or her life and the spiritual impact of faithful prayer. Does the possibility of increased joy and faith whet your spiritual appetite? "Taste and see that the Lord is good" (Psalm 34:8 NIV).

Father, make us people of prayer. Strengthen us to believe that you are listening and you do all things for good. Our trust is in you. Through Jesus our Lord. Amen.

ABOUT PRAYER

He rewards those who sincerely look for him.
—Hebrews 11:6 (Living Bible)

We were at a tiny church in a small village in Chiapas. Ostensibly, we were there to teach Vacation Bible School, but God expanded our plans. That was probably because Barbara, a veteran missionary, was with us. As we taught about prayer and made prayer chains of colored construction paper, Barbara learned that the mother helpers who had joined us knew little to nothing about prayer.

Oh, yes, they knew prayers, but they were little more than rote recitations. Barbara began to explain, in fluent Spanish, that prayer is conversation with a loving Father and that we can pray about anything. As Barbara shared in her gentle, grandmotherly way, we could see understanding and gratitude light up the beautiful faces. Before the day ended, each mother was standing with her children and praying for them for the first time ever.

There was nothing unusual about our experience in that little church. We've discovered that many of us have numerous ideas about prayer. Sometimes I would love to have a formula that guaranteed the answers I want, but could it be that I really just want to manipulate God? Is this a throwback to original sin: Do we inherently want to be God?

Deep down, we know that prayer is more than simply getting things from God; rather, prayer is about getting to know God. It's relational, developing intimacy with our Father so that more and more we trust that every detail in the life of faith is worked into something good (Romans 8:28). One of my friends says this should be followed with "eventually."

The proper order in the faith life goes something like this: Faith follows facts, and feelings catch up. When we reverse the order, we're sure to be tripped up. I must continually remind myself that my feelings aren't primary; faith embraces the facts and trusts God with the feelings.

God tells us to call him, and he answers (Jeremiah 33:3). The answers aren't always what we want, but he always responds. He tells us to ask (Matthew 7:7), and our asking is refined as we mature. When we don't receive, it's often because we don't ask or we ask for the wrong things (James 4:2–3). And God doesn't listen when there's sin in our hearts (Psalm 66:18).

I once read that prayer doesn't change things. Instead, prayer changes us, and we change things. And God is glorified.

Reflection

Someone said that we tend to treat prayer like an online shopping site. We plug in, place our order, and wait for delivery. It can be such a disappointment when the package we receive doesn't seem to fit and is definitely not what we wanted.

We may accuse God of not answering prayer when we don't like what he sends. We may even think he doesn't hear or care because he isn't indulging our selfish desires. Psalm 110:4 tells us to "enter his gates with thanksgiving and his courts with praise" (NIV). Have you considered beginning your prayers with words of gratitude? Do you then move into worship or praise?

To begin the habit of thanksgiving, try this simple exercise: Make a list of everyday reasons for thanks, such as a good night's rest, safety through the night, food for the day, satisfying relationships, responsibilities, and work for the day. Make your list as long as your imagination takes you and then begin. (Often, after we pray through our thanksgivings, we notice that our requests are fewer.)

What has been your experience with prayer?

_____

_____

How much of your prayer is given to thanksgiving?

_____

_____

Do you take time to praise?

_____

_____

What percentage of your prayer time is devoted to thanks?

_____

To praise?

_____

To petition?

_____

Father, thank you for the privilege of ongoing conversation with you. Help us to keep praying even when we don't understand or like your response. In Jesus's name. Amen.

PRAYING

God is our refuge and strength, a very present help
in trouble.

—Psalm 46:1 (KJV)

Dean was serving on a short-term mission to Guatemala. One
day, he and his colleagues headed for neighboring Honduras
to check out the status of their work there. They took a bus, hoping
to visit several mission stations.

As it happened, this was the same day the army had decided to
overthrow the government. The bus was near a police station when
a group of attackers killed twenty-one police officers. For a while
Dean's bus was held at gunpoint. Finally, the people were released,
but an opposing group later stopped them again in the rapidly
developing civil war. All day long, first one side and then the other
stopped the bus at gunpoint and then, after a while, released it. Dean
and friends arrived unharmed at their destination although they
were somewhat frazzled and hours behind schedule.

Dean later discovered that, during that wild and crazy day, his
father had been awakened at home in the states with a strong urge
to pray for him. For hours, the old saint prayed God's protection
over his son.

Across town, Dean's pastor's wife had the same experience.
Those prayer warriors wrote down when and why they prayed: it was
exactly when Dean and his friends were going through the war zone.

All our prayer needs may not be as dramatic as Dean's, but they
are still significant in God's eyes. On a recent missions trip, our
prayer team back home (essential for the success and well-being of
all ministry endeavors) was daily receiving prayer requests and being
notified of our responses. One day we asked for God's intervention

with the weather since we were conducting Vacation Bible School for a barn full of energetic young children; outdoor play was essential. The rain stopped just in time for recess. Later on the trip, we prayed for journey mercies. We could have missed our flight home, but due to the previous flight's delay, we arrived at the gate just as our group number was boarding. And God cared for one of our missioners, who drove herself alone hundreds of miles only to discover upon arriving home that she had a medical need that required hospitalization. God kept us all.

Later, we'll talk about times we think God doesn't hear our prayers. But suffice it to say, as did William Temple, Archbishop of Canterbury, "When I pray, coincidences happen, and when I don't, they don't."[8]

Reflection

Rather than debate whether or not God answers prayer, write down five verses that declare God's faithfulness in responding to our petitions:

_____

_____

_____

What does the Bible say about things that might hinder our prayers?

_____

_____

_____

Take time to talk with a prayer warrior to hear his or her experience with and thoughts about prayer.

Father, give me courage to pray more and to trust your responses. In Jesus's name. Amen.

RADICAL PRAYER

When the enemy shall come in like a flood, the Spirit
of the Lord shall lift up a standard against him.
—Isaiah 59:19 (KJV)

At a Borderland Conference, we were invited to share our
ministries and explore opportunities for collaboration. We
provide humanitarian aid to refugees as well as worship services;
however, our primary focus is the countries of origin—education,
economic, and spiritual development. We've discovered that more
people prefer to stay in their own culture and home if their needs
are met.

One of the cities in a Central American country where we
work experienced witchcraft, alcoholism, poverty, and violence that
seemed endless. Crime was so bad in that small town that it was
necessary to have four jails to house lawbreakers. Finally, church
people got desperate. They had tried every human solution, and
nothing worked.

For some, their proposal may have seemed radical, but it worked.
They prayed.

Three to four times a week, church members got together to
pray. Some even began fasting. They prayed and fasted, and they
didn't stop. Eventually, disruptive family members began coming
to faith in Jesus, and violence declined. The crime rate dropped so
dramatically that the authorities closed the jails.

As people began practicing their faith, lives, families, and
communities were transformed. People began working again, and
the economy grew. Their town is now one of the cleanest and most
prosperous in the country. When asked if they'd like to join the

caravans headed for the United States, people said there is no need to leave.

One might think the church has stopped fasting and praying, but instead, they say they need to continue so their story can be shared as encouragement that God can do what no one else can. The church meets on Saturdays for prayer vigils, and others continue to fast.

The Bible records stories of people who have encountered powerful enemies and experienced God's help as they turned to him in prayer. Once again, it's time to get radical.

Reflection

I love hearing and reading stories of God's miraculous provisions. They inspire me to ask more boldly and to trust more courageously. CS Lewis challenges us in his book *Miracles*[9] that miracles are not only possible but are far more widespread than most of us ever might have imagined. And many bookstores have selections that prompt us to become more daring in our faith lives.

What if God is who he says he is and who the great men and women of faith have proclaimed him to be? What if he is calling us to the greatest adventure of our lives by following and trusting him?

Have you ever seen something that couldn't be explained by natural laws?

_____

Have you ever asked God to do something miraculous for his sake?

_____

_____

Do a Google search about Bible verses that mention miracles. Spend some time this next week meditating on those verses and asking God to increase your faith.

Do an experiment: Set up a measurable situation (e.g., financial circumstance, relational challenge, specific guidance) and pray for a set time, expecting God's response. Some find a combination of prayer and fasting helps them focus and intensify their prayers. Pray until you are comfortable reaching out to God and trusting that he is listening. Make notes about your experience.

Father, we pray with the disciples, "Increase our faith." Amen.

THE GREATEST NAME

Signs and wonders are performed through the name
of your holy servant Jesus.

—Acts 4:30 (ESV)

When my son and daughter-in-law walked in and said they had
something to tell me, I knew this wasn't a casual visit. I sat
on one of the sofas, and they sat across from me. They had come to
tell me that my daughter had been diagnosed with leiomyosarcoma,
a rare form of cancer.

Without pausing to think, words popped out of my mouth:
"God isn't surprised."

And with that diagnosis, our family launched the support
mechanisms that families access in crisis. Some began researching
for best doctors and hospitals, others made provisions for her two
little daughters, and we all put together a prayer campaign that
spread around the world.

I sat with family members for the twelve-hour surgery that was
part of Tish's treatment regimen. With us was a sweet rabbi who
read to me a psalm that was used every day at his synagogue to
pray for Tish. Each of us passed the time in terse conversation and
responding to calls and emails for updates.

And then I received a beautiful message from a clergyman in
Rwanda. "This cancer may have a name, but we know the *greatest
name*." He had joined us in invoking that powerful name above all
names, foretold by Isaiah, asking for healing.

That was more than a decade ago. This week I will accompany
my daughter to MD Anderson for her regular checkup and to
celebrate the prayers that were answered by the One we call the
Healer. The greatest name, Emmanuel, God with us.

Reflection

In Jan Karon's *Mitford Series,* Father Timothy suggests that the prayer that is always answered is, "Thy will be done." Through deep suffering, it is hypocritical for us to pretend the pain is not deep. God knows, and his promise is that he will always be with us (Matthew 28:30), and he can be trusted with the most insurmountable circumstances (Proverbs 3:5–6). He is able to sustain us and to give us peace when we most need him (Philippians 4:6).

Jeremiah 33:3 tells us to "Call to me and I will answer you" (NIV), while Hebrews 4:16 reminds us that we can "with confidence draw near to the throne of grace, that we may receive mercy and find grace to help in time of need" (ESV). There are verses relating to healing (Jeremiah 17:14; 1 Peter 2:24; James 5:15), to provision (2 Corinthians 9:8; Matthew 6:33; Philippians 4:19), to grace (2 Corinthians 12:9–10; John 1:16–17; James 4:6), and so much more.

God's Word speaks to all our needs, and he delights in our coming to him as Father, expecting him to respond.

Can you recall a difficult circumstance when God wonderfully intervened?

_____

_____

Write a verse that brings you comfort in times of difficulty:

_____

_____

Read a biography of someone who practiced trusting prayer. Check out Hudson Taylor, or Jim Elliot. What impresses you most about prayerful people?

_____

_____

Father, all praise and glory be to you for your wonderful gift of our Lord and Savior Jesus Christ. May we center our thoughts on Emmanuel, who came to meet our deepest needs. In his name. Amen.

GROWING

Grow in the grace and knowledge of our Lord and
Savior Jesus Christ.

—2 Peter 3:18 (NIV)

At a recent teacher training orientation, one of the facilitators
said personal engagement with the Bible, God's Word, was the
single most important thing we can do for spiritual growth. Nothing
else even comes close. Pastor and theologian Tim Keller adds that
you can know the Bible without knowing God, but you cannot
know God without knowing the Bible.

When we begin a daily discipline of Bible reading, we can expect
the Holy Spirit to teach us God's truths, to point out and convict us of
sin in our lives, to correct and rebuke us in wrongdoing, and to train
us. We can also expect to be guided, encouraged, comforted, healed
emotionally and spiritually, and physically, spiritually nourished,
instructed in life and relationships, learn upright business principles,
and countless other wonders. And we can expect to grow spiritually.

But let's face it: Bible reading begins as a discipline. It requires
a commitment to take the time, to stop, to be intentional about
getting into God's presence through his Word. There really is no
excuse for not reading the Bible. In our country, there are 4.4 Bibles
in the average household. Fifty-seven percent of Americans polled
read the Bible four times a year, and only 26 percent of that group
read the Bible at least four times a week (American Bible Society).
Is it any wonder that Christianity in the global North seems to be
in decline?

I've just received a letter from someone who works in another part
of the world where Christian literature has been banned, Christian
internet has been blocked, and now Bibles cannot be purchased in

bookstores. On the other hand, it is possible to give Bibles away, and my friend and his teams distribute thousands every year to people who are eager to know God's Word.

I share these thoughts with you as we walk together because I need to be reminded of the treasure we have in the Bible and the nourishment we have through this great gift. I must remember that we all have the same number of hours in the day; we all have access to a Bible; and we will all grow by engaging with the Word. We cannot put ourselves in God's presence without being transformed. Come and go with me into the Word, and let's begin to enjoy fellowship and growth through Scripture.

Reflection

If you're new to daily devotions, you might find a modern translation of Scripture, such as The Message or The Way. The language is easy and often uses colloquial expressions. Many people enjoy reading the daily lectionary in *The Book of Common Prayer*[10], while others like devotional books, such as *My Utmost for His Highest*,[11] *God Calling*,[12] or *Daily Light on the Daily Path*.[13] *Daily Light* is a collection of Scripture for morning and evening with a theme for each.

Are you satisfied with your devotional practices?

_____

_____

With your study of Scripture?

_____

What is your favorite Bible study/book?

_____

Why?

_____

If you don't regularly read a portion of Scripture, assign a week where you spend some time each day reading from John's or Matthew's gospels. Record what the reading says to you personally and what action you might take in response to what you've read.

_____

_____

_____

Begin reading the Word and watch yourself grow.

Father, please remind me that the entrance of your word gives light. Help me to pursue you with all my heart. In Jesus's name. Amen.

STRENGTH

Finally, be strong in the Lord and in his mighty power.

—Ephesians 6:10 (NIV)

The youngest member of the team was looking forward to his seventieth birthday; the oldest was nearing seventy-seven; and all others were somewhere in between. More like a herd of dinosaurs than dynamic missionary workers. And all the assignments with which we were tasked included hard manual labor: hauling trash, digging drainage ditches, installing an irrigation system, or digging large holes for planting trees and berry bushes. I didn't mention that all but two team members were retired professionals who had spent their working lives sitting at a desk or conferring or researching.

Every evening I prayed for strength to continue the next day and for no one to be injured. One of our team members had arrived with a compression bandage on his knee in preparation for surgery; another had his right arm in a sling; a third had a condition known as trigger finger. You get the idea. A motley crew. Yet all our tasks were completed; no one was sidelined, and there were no injuries.

On the night prior to heading home, one of our teammates confessed that at the end of the first day he thought he would have to ask if he could leave early because of his exhaustion and strain. And then he prayed for strength for one more day. At the end of that day he thought for sure he'd have to leave, but he prayed for strength—for one more day. And he made it. All through the week he prayed, and he found that at the end of the mission, he was stronger than ever.

God promises us, "As thy days, so shall thy strength be" (Deuteronomy 33:25 KJV). Let's embrace this not only for our physical needs but our spiritual, emotional, and mental needs. When we want strength to persevere or to address a difficult task, we read, "I can do all this through him who gives me strength" (Philippians 4:13 NIV); "So do not fear, for I am with you; do not be dismayed, for I am your God. I will strengthen you and help you; I will uphold you with my righteous right hand" (Isaiah 41:10 NIV); and one of my favorites, "But those who hope in the Lord will renew their strength. They will soar on wings like eagles; they will run and not grow weary, they will walk and not be faint" (Isaiah 40:31 NIV).

With these and so many more precious promises, there's no need for us to lag or fear when all we have to do is access what has already been given us.

Reflection

Dietrich Bonhoeffer encouraged the young seminarians at Finkenwalde Seminary to live according to Jesus's teachings from the Sermon on the Mount. Among their daily disciplines, the young men were expected to spend time meditating on the Word so that their lives would be directed and informed by the Living Word, Jesus Christ.

As holistic beings, we are nourished by daily intake of Scripture, with meditation being an integral component of Christian growth. We locate verses that inform the need of the moment, and we learn what God says.

With the need for strength, here is just a smattering of scriptures to which we can refer: "strengthen me according to your word" (Psalms 119:28 NIV). "He gives strength to the weary and increases the power of the weak" (Isaiah 40:29 NIV). "I will strengthen you and help you; I will uphold you with my righteous right hand" (Isaiah 41:10 NIV). "I can do all this through him who gives me strength" (Philippians 4:13 NIV). "The joy of the Lord is your strength" (Nehemiah 8:10 KJV). God has given us his Word to address all our needs.

Practice meditation this week and note how it affects you. Jot down the results of this discipline:

_____

_____

_____

Father, we acknowledge you as the source of energy, inspiration, and strength. Let your will be done through these weak vessels. In Jesus's name. Amen.

HE'S DEPENDABLE

Cast all your anxiety on him because he cares for you.

—1 Peter 5:7 (NIV)

Betty, our former missions director, confessed that she is descended from a long line of cautious people who are anxious when facing a new situation. Her father, the classic example, made the family bring their empty suitcases to him the day before a road trip to make sure they would fit in the trunk of the car.

Picture Betty's anxiety level when facing her first mission trip. She was worried because she was the team leader and had no experience. She had never been to the place where the team was going in Mexico to teach Vacation Bible School; she had never taught VBS; she spoke very little Spanish; and she was expected to write the curriculum. What could go wrong?

At this point, you can image that Betty's stress was so intense that she almost decided not to go. She went to a good friend and shared her fears. With her friend's help and prayer, Betty realized God really did care for her and wanted her to trust him enough to step out in faith, giving him all her anxieties. So, holding tightly to this reassurance, she led the team into what turned out to be a glorious adventure filled with joy, blessings, and some wonderful spiritual surprises.

Betty discovered that God provided creative ways to address issues with the team. For example, after several days away from home, the young girls approached her with their concerns about the lack of water to shampoo their long tresses. In a first-world environment with abundant water, these girls had grown up daily shampooing their hair and were deeply distressed with the lack of proper hygiene. Not about to be defeated this far into the mission, Betty went into town, rented a hotel room, and provided a blissful spa afternoon for her girls. Refreshed and satisfied, the girls were ready to again share their love and gifts with the village children. Betty became the go-to person for all things missional as she learned to cast her cares on the Lord.

The church returned to that place in Mexico for many years and formed lasting relationships that are still treasured today. Now when Betty goes on a mission, she holds this thought in her heart: "When there is nothing left but God, you find that God is all you need." Philippians 4:6–7 says, "Do not be anxious about anything but in everything, by prayer and petition with thanksgiving, present your requests to God. And the peace of God will guard your hearts and your minds in Jesus Christ" (NIV).

Reflection

Anxiety, stress, and fear are all cut from the same cloth. Could it be that we don't believe ourselves capable of the challenges facing us in new ventures? Or could it be that we don't think God is able to empower us for the challenges we face?

Imagine handing a computer tech your iPad that continues to malfunction. Just as he's about to leave with a promise that he'll call when the machine is repaired, you stop him and pull the iPad from his hands. You feel silly because you know it doesn't work, and you have no idea how to correct the problem, so you hand it back. And the action is repeated. It's just hard to let go.

More than likely, this wouldn't happen in real life because we pretty much know our limits. But spiritually, it's sometimes hard to trust God to do what we can't. It's an admission that we're not in control, so how could he be? But what if he really can give us that peace that passes understanding as we release our cares to him?

Try this exercise next time you're tempted to be anxious: Imagine your cares are in your hands, and give them to Christ. Then let go and walk away. Each time you want to take that annoying trouble back, repeat the action. Make a list of chronic worries that plague you and practice handing them over to our Lord. With intention and repetition, *the peace of God will guard your heart and mind in Christ Jesus.*

Father, you are God, and we are not. Help us remember that to guard our hearts and live in your peace. In Jesus's name. Amen.

LITTLE THINGS

Shew me a token for good ... because thou, Lord,
hast holpen me, and comforted me.
                                        —Psalm 86:17 (KJV)

It was my first transatlantic flight, and I'd never flown for hours suspended in a small silver tube over the water. For whatever irrational reason, I honestly felt safer flying over land than over the ocean, but there was no way we could bypass the water and arrive in Europe.

Our destination was Ireland. The allure of the Emerald Isle should have dispelled any anxieties I was experiencing. I threw myself into preparations, thinking that would alleviate my apprehension. Still, I couldn't rid myself of that nagging fear, and I was too embarrassed to admit I was nervous about such a silly matter.

Denial didn't take away the trepidation. Busy-ness didn't cure my concerns. Prayer didn't seem to bring relief. All I could do was simply admit my weakness and ask God to somehow take away all the stress I was experiencing.

The night before we were to leave, an insignificant and mysterious event occurred. I stepped into the shower before going to bed and was surprised by the most wonderful and distinct scent. Someone, I still don't know who, had placed a bar of Irish Spring soap into the soap dish, which permeated the atmosphere with hope, joy, and reassurance. I knew instantly that it would be a wonderful, safe trip.

Nowadays I spend days and nights on planes going to various ministries around the world, and I am always grateful for God's patience in giving me little things to assure me that he is in control.

That he doesn't laugh at my weaknesses or fears. Instead, he cures them. Lovingly, he prepares me for what he has prepared for me.

And he does that for us all. When we own our weaknesses, we find that his grace is sufficient (2 Corinthians 12:9) and that he helps and comforts us.

Reflections

The Bible has a curious story about Gideon, a fearful man God called to be a military leader of his people. There's a touch of humor in the telling of his story, for when the angel first meets Gideon, he calls him a mighty warrior—this Gideon, who's threshing wheat in a winepress to hide from his enemies (Judges 6). Instead of criticizing his lack of faith, the angel recognizes Gideon as God sees him.

Imagine the exploits we would do if we didn't bemoan our weaknesses and failures as we see them and, instead, embrace the person God is creating us to be. How liberating to see ourselves as God sees us and to trust his working in us.

Do you ever struggle with fears that seem foolish?

_____

_____

_____

Consider thanking God for unmasking the fear; asking him to strengthen you to confront the fear; recognizing that he is greater than any fear you will ever have; and accepting his freedom from fear.

Sing hymns that build your confidence in God, such as "It Is Well with My Soul," "Be Still My Soul," or "In Christ Alone." There are few things that drive away doubts and fears like singing. Sing aloud and sing loudly.

Father, thank you for your patience. Help us discard our fears even as we embrace your provisions. In Jesus our Lord. Amen.

FINDING JOY

And all thy children shall be taught of the Lord.
—Isaiah 54:13 (KJV)

D o you have any special practices that ensure you consistently
maintain joy? I'm not speaking about *happy-clappy* pretensions
of pleasure. I'm thinking of that peace and quietness that help us
through the most difficult of circumstances. I find that so many of
the lessons I learn are from the young people around me.

When my daughter left for college, she went with two
admonitions: "Remember whose you are," and "Get a job." Work
was nothing new to Tish, but we realized that finding a job in a small
college town might be a challenge. We prayed.

The first week of school, Tish was recruited by a student whose
boss was looking for help. From semester to semester, she found work
and learned to pray through school and job problems. When work
was scarce in her senior year, Tish went to the school placement office
and was hired on the spot by the manager, who needed a babysitter.

One evening, Tish called to chat and tell me about an experience
with her new job. "There's been so much to do around here with the
children and both the parents so busy. I've started helping out with
the house and laundry. Mom, there was so much ironing, I knew it
would take hours. And then I remembered how we always used to
sing while we worked. I pulled out the ironing board and sang one
song after another as I ironed, and the work seemed so much easier
and was finished before I knew it.

"And you know what, Mom? I felt happy that I could do it.
Singing really works. And you should've seen their faces when they
came home," Tish concluded.

With that little story I was ready to sing myself.

Reflection

Have you noticed how many of our hymns come from the Psalms? For example, we sing "What Wondrous Love Is This?," "Jesus Shall Reign," "On Eagle's Wings," and many others. And in the field of psychosocial behavior, singing has been shown to increase positive emotions and reduce fatigue and stress.

Copy the words to some of your favorite hymns and begin to use those in times of distress or unease.

_____

_____

_____

_____

Prior to your morning or evening times of devotion, sing. Sing your songs of praise, thanksgiving, or prayer.

_____

_____

_____

Note how singing affects your prayers, your attitude, your emotions:

_____

_____

Father, I've heard it said that music is the only thing we will take with us from earth to heaven. Help me to keep a song in my heart. In Jesus's name. Amen.

WORDS

May these words of my mouth and this meditation
of my heart be pleasing in your sight, Lord, my
Rock and my Redeemer.

—Psalm 19:14 (NIV)

You've likely heard the saying, "Sticks and stones may break my bones, but words will never hurt me." This was first cited in 1862 and was an encouragement to ignore taunts and criticism intended to wound. That may be very well in a rhyme, but the truth is, words can hurt. Poet Will Carleton wrote, "Thoughts unexpressed may sometimes fall back dead, but God himself can't kill them when they're said."[14]

There is a Jewish fable about a rabbi who took the local gossip to the top of a mountain along with his feather pillow. The gossipy man was told to cut the pillow open and to shake it in the wind. Strong gusts carried the feathers near and far, and then the rabbi instructed the man to pick up all the feathers. "They are just like the words that come from your mouth," the rabbi said. "The wind carries them hither and thither, and they can never be retrieved."

But there are also words of love and affirmation, of approval and admiration, of support and encouragement, and any number of words that bless. Those words are like "apples of gold in settings of silver" (Proverbs 25:11 ESV). We all love those kinds of words.

Amy Carmichael,[15] missionary to India, had a little test (she called this the three sieves) for conversation: Is it true? Is it kind? Is it necessary? Some things may be true or they may be kind but may be totally unnecessary to repeat. This last sieve may be the most difficult test to pass as it seems so easy to repeat information that others don't need. That especially applies to truth that would be hurtful if divulged.

How wonderful to be able to shower someone with words that bless and lift. They don't have to be profound or abundant. Just a few heartfelt words can make a person's day—or bring healing to a broken spirit. What a lovely discipline to develop: handing out "apples of gold" today and then, tomorrow, doing the same thing until kind, true, and necessary words become our habit.

Reflection

When I think of the things that proceed from our mouths, I'm not surprised that James says the tongue is set on fire of hell (James 3:6). That's a rather severe indictment but true, nevertheless.

I'm discovering that the more I guard my thoughts, the easier it is to monitor my words. For example, we know that one role of the Holy Spirit is to convict us of sin—even our uncharitable thoughts. When I become critical or harbor negative judgments about others, God's Spirit lasers in on that and reminds me of his mercy and forgiveness. He reminds me that my calling is to be loving, which begins in my heart.

What verses remind you to watch what you say?

_____

_____

_____

_____

Write a prayer asking God's help in making your conversations those that lift up and enrich your hearers:

_____

_____

_____

_____

Father, help me to put a watch over my mouth that I only speak words that bless. In Jesus's name. Amen.

PROTECTED

For he will command his angels concerning you to
guard you in all your ways; they will lift you up in
their hands, so that you will not strike your foot
against a stone.

—Psalm 91:11–12 (NIV)

My brother was a Green Beret on the frontlines the whole time
he served in Vietnam. Every day our family prayed the 91st
Psalm, which promises protection from so many types of danger:
night terrors, pestilence, lions and serpents, and even tripping on
rocks. And Jack would remind his platoon that people were praying
for them. We heard tales of close calls and firsthand reports of life in
a war zone. And we also heard tales of God's faithfulness. It was a joy
and relief when Jack was delivered home safely after his tour of duty.

Often we look for second meanings in Scripture, as described by
CS Lewis, and are aware that the dangers we encounter daily may
be of a different nature than either of the Psalms mentioned above.
But these dangers can threaten us to the eternal peril of our spirits:
anxiety that God is preoccupied just when we need him; sleepless
nights due to all sorts of worries; the hidden presence of pandemics;
and multiple insecurities. *These* are the everyday enemies against
which we most likely need protection.

Julian of Norwich (1342–1416) lived through the Black Plague
and the Peasants' Revolt (aka Wat Tyler's Rebellion or the Great
Rising), spending much of her life in seclusion in a small cell (room)
attached to one of the churches in Norwich. Julian, to whom many
came for counseling and prayer, was known for writing, "All shall
be well, and all manner of thing shall be well." Even though she
lived through some of England's and the world's darkest times, her

trust in God's goodness brought assurance to those who sought her wisdom.

Think of all the verses God has provided for our encouragement in times like these: "God is our refuge and strength, an ever-present help in trouble" (Psalm 46:1 NIV). "My God is my rock, in whom I take refuge, my shield and the horn of my salvation" (2 Samuel 22:3 NIV). "You are my hiding place, you will protect me from trouble and surround me with songs of deliverance" (Psalm 32:7 NIV). "Even though I walk through the darkest valley, I will fear no evil, for you are with me; your rod and your staff, they comfort me" (Psalm 23:4 NIV). And then, Ephesians 6:10–18 reminds us to put on God's armor for protection from the enemy.

No matter what our circumstance, "His divine power has given us everything we need" (2 Peter 1:3 NIV). God is faithful. "The one who chose you can be trusted, and he will do this" (1 Thessalonians 5:24 Contemporary English Version).

Reflection

One of the benefits of Scripture memorization is that God's Word is accessible wherever we are at whatever time. For example, while driving home alone on a dark night, we could remind ourselves that, "Even though I walk through the darkest valley, I will fear no evil, for you are with me" (Psalm 23:4 NIV) or "The angel of the Lord encamps around those who fear him, and he delivers them" (Psalm 34:7 NIV), or "But the Lord is faithful, and he will strengthen you and protect you from the evil one" (2 Thessalonians 3:3 NIV).

If you are regularly confronted with unwarranted fears, consider meditating on one of the many verses in the Bible that address fear. Take a journal or notepad and write what the verse is saying; put your name at the beginning of the verse, recognizing that it is addressed to you personally. Pray to be set free from fear.

Can you recall times when you were aware (perhaps in hindsight) that you were divinely protected?

_____

_____

Remember to thank God for his protection.

Father, outside you, there is no place of safety. Let us hide ourselves in you. Amen.

REGARDING TEMPTATION

Jesus said to him, "Away from me, Satan!"
—Matthew 4:10 (NIV)

I gave myself a holiday, which happened to coincide with the spring break of my young grandchildren. Since they're both rather artistic, I thought a trip to the local craft store would be a big hit, and I was right. En route, William warned that the store would be packed with all the *Breakers*, but we finally determined it would be worth the risk. To our happy surprise, we were so early, almost no one but the *partners* were there.

The game rules had been predetermined. Everyone would decide what special thing he or she would select, and then we'd hit the aisles. William knew immediately what he wanted, but he politely suggested that Caroline, his younger sister, might need a little longer to decide and that we should let her go first.

It didn't take Caroline long to select a build-it-yourself tent and bedroll for her American Girl doll. And then she did something unexpected: Caroline turned her head and covered her eyes, saying, "There are so many things that I like, I don't want to see any more." William selected a helicopter kit, and we led Caroline, hand still covering her eyes, to the cash register.

I wish temptation were that easy to resist. On the other hand, perhaps it is—we just don't cover our eyes, and we're not that determined to avoid it. One of my clergy friends told me he'd never seen a temptation he didn't like. That's really the nature of temptation—something we like or desire but intuitively know it's not for our good or God's glory. (Why go to a donut shop when you're trying to lose weight?) "God is faithful; he will not let you be tempted beyond what you can bear. But when you are tempted, he will also provide a way out so that you can endure it" (1 Corinthians 10:13 NIV).

Caroline reminded me of something important: while God can provide a way out of temptation, I have to cooperate by turning away from those things that can trip me up and even lead me off the pathway. Way to go, little one.

Reflection

Proverbs 23:7 says, "For as he thinketh in his heart, so is he" (KJV). Those things that occupy our minds tend to direct our actions. What is the central focus of your thought life?

_____

_____

_____

Do you ever find yourself dealing with a specific temptation? Can you identify that bothersome problem?

_____

_____

_____

In 1952, Norman Vincent Peale published a book that became an instant best-seller. _The Power of Positive Thinking_[16] emphasized the spiritual strength we have through disciplining our thoughts to "rise above the obstacles that might defeat [us]." Peale encouraged his readers to utilize their thoughts to "produce a victorious life" no matter what their life circumstances.

As people of faith, we have been told that everyone suffers similar temptations but that God will help us bear, rather than be overcome by temptation (1 Corinthians 10:13). What are some practical ways we can overcome temptation?

_____

_____

_____

If you were asked to advise someone who is struggling with temptation, what would you say?

_____

_____

_____

Father, thank you that we can call on you in times of trouble or temptation and expect your response. Amen.

TOO MUCH

> Lay not up for yourselves treasures upon earth, where moth and rust doth corrupt, and where thieves break through and steal: But lay up for yourselves treasures in heaven, where neither moth nor rust doth corrupt, and where thieves do not break through nor steal: For where your treasure is, there will your heart be also.
>
> Matthew 6:19–21 (KJV)

On his latest visit, my Ethiopian friend Getch was confounded by the proliferation of storage units throughout our city. *Whatever are they for?* he wondered.

It was difficult for me to explain that Americans have so much stuff that they have to rent additional space to warehouse it. In the whole continent of Africa where most people are happy just to have daily food for their families, the idea of excess was incomprehensible to Getch. And it was a little difficult for me to justify the situation.

In the Bible, Jesus is approached by a man who wants him to convince his brother to divide an inheritance. Rather than side with the offended man, Jesus says that life doesn't consist of an abundance of things (not what the brother wanted to hear). Jesus goes on to tell the story of the rich man whose harvest was so great, his barns couldn't hold everything. Instead of opening the barn doors and inviting the poor and needy to help themselves, the rich man decided to tear down the structures and build larger barns so that he could sit back and enjoy his wealth. Jesus calls him a fool. Life isn't about things.

Have you ever wrecked your dream car? Or had moths eat holes into an expensive Asian rug? (Ask me how I know.) Or had someone accidently break a treasured piece of porcelain? Life isn't about things. When someone broke an item in the home of Corrie ten Boom, a saintly woman whose family sheltered Jews during World War II, she said it didn't matter, it didn't have eternal life.

When you're planning to travel, one of the first things that must be considered is *how little do I need?* The missioners I know who struggle most with packing (and living) are those who are thinking, *What if?* Ministry is not about what we carry with us but what we carry in us. The basis of all *what ifs?* is worry, not trust. Plan, pray, pack, and then go.

Life isn't about things. God said he takes care of the things (Matthew 6:25–30).

Reflections

Research indicates that materialistic people suffer higher levels of anxiety, depression, and substance abuse. They are less happy and experience fewer positive emotions than their peers. I wonder if that could be why so many missioners speak of greater joy among those they serve in emerging nations than what they see at home? For sure, when those same missionaries describe the people among whom they work, typically one of the top characteristics mentioned is joy.

How would you describe yourself when considering the topic of materialism?

_____

_____

_____

A young man is introduced in the Bible as the "rich young ruler." He eagerly sought Jesus and wanted a deeper relationship with God. "What should I do?" he asked Jesus. Knowing his overarching interest, Jesus told him to sell everything and give to the poor. (Notice he doesn't tell everyone to do that.) Scripture says Jesus loved him (Mark 10:21), but he let him go. The young man was more interested in his things than in the true riches from God.

What do you imagine would have happened if the young fellow had sold everything?

_____

_____

_____

What would you do?

_____

_____

_____

Father, we are so blessed, and it's sometimes hard to let go. Fill us with such gratitude that we joyously open our hearts and hands to those in need—just as you did and do with us. In Jesus's name. Amen.

TREASURES

It is the blessing of the Lord that makes rich, and
He adds no sorrow to it.
—Proverbs 10:22 (New American Standard Bible)

M ost countries in which we work are desperately impoverished,
but many of the people there would never accept being
labeled poor. And in truth, their dependence on Christ Jesus renders
them rich indeed.

On one of my assignments in East Africa, a missionary gifted me
with a beautiful handwoven basket filled with all sorts of necessities.
There were fruit, a type of margarine, liquid disinfectant, mosquito
repellant, and a bar of blue soap, among other things. I was intrigued
by the soap. It was a sort of industrial grade wedge that had obviously
been cut off a larger piece.

The blue cleaning product, like nothing I had seen at home, was
for scrubbing floors and washing dishes and clothes. It was not to
be used for bathing or shampooing due to its chemical composition.
In the village markets there was nothing else suitable for bathing.
Those products were available in the capital city and were considered
luxury items. Village people simply could not afford hand soap. This
is perhaps why 64 percent of the people in that East African country
do not wash their hands with soap and water (and may explain why
so many diseases affect the population).

One afternoon, I was in a brainstorming session with the
regional director of education, and we discussed ideas for motivating
young students in the scholarship program. We spoke of various
strategies, and then I asked if we might host a dinner for students
who had excelled along with their families. I watched the director
as he processed the possibility, and then his face lighted up. His eyes

twinkled and he said, "And we could give each of them … a bar of hand soap." It was agreed.

All the regional students who do well in this next year's studies will be hosted at a special dinner for them and their families. As their achievements are read and they are introduced, each will be presented with their own scented, olive oil infused bar of hand soap. Sheer luxury and a well-deserved award for outstanding students.

A real treasure.

Reflections

The story about another culture obviously refers to a temporal product that has value due to its scarcity in that area. Could it be that the thing that holds our heart is our treasure? (Matthew 6:21) We're not told that we cannot own material things. In fact, 1 Timothy 6:17 reminds us that he gives us all things to enjoy.

What is your treasure?

_____

_____

In your list, was anything eternal mentioned?

_____

_____

What treasures do you now possess that you can transport to heaven?

_____

_____

_____

Does your treasure chest need editing?

_____

_____

Father, if heaven weren't our future and your everyday blessings a reality, knowing and enjoying you every single day is enough. Thank you. Amen.

STUMBLING AROUND

3

STUMBLING AROUND

It would be reassuring to think that once we begin this legendary journey of faith, the path would be shiny and clear of obstacles and enemies, and joy would be our constant companion.

Are you surprised by the deterrents on the path? Have you found that they really work together for good?

MORE THAN

But my God shall supply all your need according to
his riches in glory by Christ Jesus.

—Philippians 4:19 (KJV)

After being a college "stop-out" for twelve years, I needed to
get back in school and desperately needed a student loan to
finish those last two years. I filled out the application, mailed it in,
and prayed, hoping to be approved. After all, we were living under
the official poverty line, and a degree would enhance my ability to
provide.

By faith and with a small gift from my dad, I entered university,
studying after the children were in bed and doing projects when
they were away. My professor assured me that I was doing well—all
I needed were funds for tuition.

With midsemester closing in, it was time to register for spring.
I was anxious to hear from the lending agency, but I was confident
that I qualified for the loan. When the packet arrived, I eagerly
ripped it open, keen to share the good news. Instead, I learned that
my application had been rejected.

Unimaginable grief tore at my soul. This was a dream I was
convinced God had for me. It was the answer to everything—
provision, profession, opportunity, the future. The letter had to be
a mistake.

I wept and wept in disbelief until there were no tears left. Finally,
I took the odious letter to my bedroom, tossed it on the bed, and
lay down beside it. I'd heard about relinquishment; now was my
opportunity to practice it. "Father, if one semester is all you want
for me, I give my dream to you," I said with a moan. Then came
the stillness.

I went to class the next day, and responding to an impulse, I dropped in to see my advisor.

"I've been looking for you," she said. "I want you to interview for a job at St. Luke's."

I protested, reminding her that I didn't yet have a degree, but she was insistent. She called the school, and they asked that I come right away.

I did the interview, and as we finished our conversation, the early childhood coordinator said, almost as an afterthought, "If we hire you, we will pay your tuition until you finish your degree."

I drove home in a daze and arrived in time to answer the phone. Another university department was calling to offer a job. When I opened my mail, I read that a presidential scholarship was mine for the spring semester.

I taught many years at St. Luke's, and they did, indeed, pay my tuition (along with other scholarships) all the way through my master's degree. I had wanted a loan—God gave me a scholarship.

Reflection

Evelyn Underhill, teacher and writer from the last century, said, "Humility and love ... are essential for successful prayer."[17] When we pray specifically for a certain thing, do you think we are being humble?

_____

In this story, would you say God answered prayer?

_____

If yes, how?

_____

_____

If no, how do you explain the scholarships?

_____

Do you think we limit God with our demands?

_____

Father, your ways are so much higher than ours. Help us to trust you in all things, even when it seems that nothing is working the way we've planned. Thank you that your provisions are infinite, and your gifts are abundant. Amen.

NO CONVENIENT TIMES

My times are in your hands.

—Psalm 31:15 (NIV)

W hen I was newly returned to university, I struggled to balance parenting as a single mother, two jobs, and college requirements. It took all the energy and grace I could muster to address each responsibility in a fairly adequate manner and still ensure my own spiritual and mental health.

The daily routine left no wiggle room: breakfast for everyone, school drop-offs, on to work, pick-ups, dinner and homework, night classes, and bedtime, and then it was my turn to do school assignments. In addition, there were music, Brownie meetings, and sports. And then one of the children had a minor crisis in school— just as I was preparing for a midterm exam. I talked with sympathetic teachers to resolve the issue, and then I spoke to my university professor. I thought it only reasonable to see if my midterm exam could be rescheduled so that I could take the challenges one at a time. That made perfect sense to me.

I made an appointment with my professor to plead my case, but Dr. Waldron would have none of it.

She said something I've never forgotten. "Marthe, you will find that life doesn't stop to allow for crises. There are no convenient times for problems. Everything flows together. It's up to you to handle everything *as it comes*."

She didn't tell me how to do it, but the bottom line was that I couldn't postpone the exam until it was convenient. And I wouldn't be able to slow down time for my personal accommodation.

This was possibly one of the best lessons I learned in that early childhood development class. Life comes at us fast, and the only way to stay poised and at peace with the stresses that make up every single day is to invite Christ into every situation. We can pray for guidance, wisdom, and grace. We can ask for help in setting priorities. And, "in every situation, by prayer and petition, with thanksgiving, [we can] present [our] requests to God. And the peace of God, which transcends all understanding, will guard [our] hearts and ... minds in Christ Jesus" (Philippians 4:6–7 NIV) I couldn't manage or control the circumstances that intruded into my life, but with Christ's help, I could manage *myself* with regard to the circumstances. It worked.

Thank you very much, Dr. Waldron.

Reflection

My professor said that there were no convenient times for crisis. Have you ever had that experience? Have you ever experienced God's help during such events?

_____

_____

_____

What directions for addressing difficult life issues are found in Philippians 4:6–7?

_____

_____

_____

Sweet Lord, you see the end from the beginning, and nothing ever takes you by surprise. Forgive us when we complain. You know exactly what we can bear and are there to strengthen us or to carry the load when we can't. Thank you. Amen.

MAKING IT

Therefore, encourage one another and build each
other up, just as in fact you are doing.
—1 Thessalonians 5:11 (NIV)

I had noticed the sweatshirt earlier when we were exploring
Pompeii and asked the obvious question, "So you're a Razorback?"

"Yes, I am," the young lady replied.

"And we're from Arkansas," her mother added. Diane then
boasted of the athletic prowess of her two daughters, as would any
proud mother. They swiftly blended into the crowd of hikers.

Pompeii continues to impress, particularly after the fairly
recent eruptions of Kilauea in Hawaii and Volcán de Fuego in
Guatemala. I studied volcanology in university and was interested
in the archeological site, but the opportunity to hike to the top of
Vesuvius was especially intriguing. I didn't realize how challenging
the incline would be for me.

We'd been warned that the first part of the climb would be hard,
and I thought I could disregard a recent pulmonary condition. My
two grandchildren and I started the hike together, but the further
we climbed, the harder it was for me to keep up, and I was gasping
for breath.

That's when Diane, my new friend from Arkansas, overtook
me. "You go on up. I'll climb with your grandmother," she told my
grandchildren.

I knew the youngsters, like racehorses, were ready to bolt, but
they hesitated to leave me.

"Go," Diane urged. "I'll climb with her."

So we climbed. We hiked a few yards and rested. Then we gained
a few more yards and stopped. Diane never proposed that I give

up. She never criticized me or told me I needed to go back down. Instead, she was my companion as we inched our way to the top. We were almost there when we saw two Razorbacks running toward us.

They saw me and yelled, "You're almost there. You can do it." And with their mom, we made it, the four of us.

At the summit, I found my grandchildren. Moreover, I saw the caldera and the steam making its way through the cracks in Vesuvius's massive crater. And because of a compassionate stranger, I had made it to the top.

Reflection

Can you recall an incident when someone befriended you during a challenging time?

_____

Do you prefer to give or to receive?

_____

Is it hard to receive from others?

_____

What characteristic might be hindering your receiving?

_____

Might this be worth serious processing? If so, what steps can be taken to address this spiritual problem?

_____

_____

_____

In times of struggle, try to remember that Jesus told us to "bear one another's burdens" (Galatians 6:2 ESV). There will always be opportunities in our lives to pay it forward.

Father, thank you for bringing saints into our lives with compassionate hearts. Make me like them. Amen.

WHAT HAPPENED?

Abide in me, and I in you. As the branch cannot bear fruit of itself, except it abide in the vine; no more can ye, except ye abide in me.

—John 15:4 (KJV)

Reggie was a beautiful little four-year old—curly blond hair and vibrant blue eyes—a real charmer. Happily, by the time he got to my class, I had a few years of teaching under my belt and was certified to work with special-needs children on all places of the spectrum.

In our first parent conference, Reggie's caring parents asked if I would be willing to work with the psychologists who were overseeing Reggie's developmental and behavioral issues. Of course, I wanted to do what I could to get this little person on track.

At first, it was really easy. With small classes, my aide and I kept an eye on Reggie, made notations on his chart every five minutes, and encouraged him to participate appropriately. For a few weeks and with our guidance, he was a model student.

Then one day it happened. I was teaching, when Reggie suddenly exploded, shot out of his chair, and began jumping on tables and overturning empty chairs. I looked at my aide, and she immediately ushered the other students from the room while I coaxed Reggie to sit and talk. Finally, the little blonde tornado was quiet.

"Reggie," I said, "you've had so many good days, and you've been doing so well. What happened?"

Without hesitation, Reggie responded, penitently, "Teacher, I ran out of nice."

Immediately, I understood. There would be other rough times when Reggie ran out of nice, but by year's end, there were no more outbursts. I've learned that through successive years and loving support, Reggie has developed into a delightful young man. He even serves on his church's ministry team.

When I run out of nice myself, I try to remember Reggie. I remind myself that there isn't any good thing in my flawed humanity but only what Christ produces in and through me. So I sometimes need to make U-turns to get back to the source that never runs out.

Reflection

Tim Keller says we run into trouble when we blame others for our unacceptable behavior. We blame our heritage, our genes, circumstances, and any number of things for who we are rather than seeking our identity in Christ. Keller goes on to say that when we seek affirmation from a person rather than the divine, it reinforces the notion that we've given people the authority to determine who we will be rather than God.

Paul's letter to the Galatians is all about freedom from the bondages in our lives, bondages that may occur even without our conscious knowledge, such as a certain temperament, a long held grudge, an irrational fear, or any other thing that binds us. List anything that robs your joy or peace.

_____

_____

_____

Pray specifically for Christ's freedom (Galatians 5:1).

Father, remind me that I can do all things through Christ who strengthens me. In Jesus's name. Amen.

THE BEST DAY

And he shall turn the heart of the fathers to the children.

—Malachi 4:6 (KJV)

He was playing ice hockey when another player ran into him and broke his leg. The little guy was patched up and spent the remainder of the day in bed with a cast.

Some days later, his teacher asked the class to tell about the best day of their lives. When it came time for this youngster to share, he said, "It was the day I broke my leg."

The teacher interrupted, saying, "You didn't understand. I asked you to tell about the best day of your life."

Again, the little fellow said, "It was the day I broke my leg. That was the day my daddy spent the whole day with me."

To this day, the father cannot tell the story without tearing up. He says it was a wakeup call. He had been leaving the house at five o'clock every morning and coming home when it was dark. His children hadn't needed all the things he provided; they needed him.

Children tend to base the image of their heavenly Father on what they know of their earthly father. In all learning, we move from the concrete to the abstract, and it is so spiritually. We learn unconditional love from our earthly father; we observe his character traits and assign those to our heavenly Father; we believe that our heavenly Father accepts us in the same measure as our earthly father. All the traits, temperaments, dispositions, characteristics, and values that we see demonstrated by our earthly father we transfer to our heavenly Father. True or not.

It's no wonder that our children sometimes have trouble relating to God as one who has pursued them with everlasting love (Jeremiah

31:3), who will never leave or forsake them (Deuteronomy 31:6), who always keeps his promises (Joshua 21:45), and who has good plans for them (Jeremiah 29:11). But there's no need to despair. As long as we're alive, there's time to love and to heal. God has given us the marvelous promise to restore the years the locusts have eaten (Joel 2:25), and we can apply that as we reach out in love to our children. With our cooperation, God can heal old wounds and turn our children's hearts to him and to us.

Reflections

I've not met the perfect person. I know many people who want to be perfect but still walk around in fleshly bodies that know disappointment.

The father in this story had no intention of causing grief while he was intently focused on providing for his family and working long hours to do so. Have you ever experienced an aha moment when you recognized the unintended grief your behavior had imposed on someone? Or have you had the joy of reconciliation when a friend or colleague bridged a gap that had occurred unknowingly? What impact did either of these events have on you?

_____

_____

_____

On your loved one?

_____

_____

_____

Ask God to open your eyes to see how you are perceived by your family, friends, and colleagues. See if there might be a need for repentance.

Thank you, Father, for showing us your love through Jesus Christ. Make us the parents and grandparents you'd have us be and use us to bring healing. In Jesus, our Lord. Amen.

UNPARDONABLE

But if you do not forgive others their sins, your
Father will not forgive your sins.

—Matthew 6:15 (NIV)

G K Chesterton writes a provocative story[18] in his Father Brown
series about an occurrence among a small clique of close
friends, a group, such as ones traveling with us on our own journey.
One has challenged another to a duel, and when a death results, the
killer flees into exile. After many years, the friends learn that the
runaway has returned but refuses to reenter society. There is much
talk about forgiveness and the justification of the duel (which was
legal in those days).

The well-intended friends discuss how best to coerce their friend
to leave his isolation even as Father Brown cautions against it. Finally,
they force the recluse's hand, only to discover that the living person
is actually the one thought to have been killed. The dead friend was
essentially murdered by the living.

The little group is incensed. (One friend they could forgive
but not the other.) Brown chastises them, saying they forgive only
those sins (and sinners) that they think are not really sins (such as a
duel) while tolerating "conventional" wrongs. Someone protests that
what was done was vile, and Brown counters with, "[L]eave [me]
to console those who really need consolation; who do things really
indefensible, things that neither the world nor they themselves can
defend; and none but a priest will pardon. Leave us with the men
who commit the mean and revolting and real crimes; mean as St.
Peter when the cock crew, and yet the dawn came."

By twos and threes, the friends leave in silence. In the story,
Chesterton is not pardoning the killer, he is forgiving him—while

pointing out the hypocrisy of his "friends" who were selective in their pardon.

Do we ever qualify sin? This sin is worse than that—this is nothing while that is heinous and unforgivable. "If you, Lord, kept a record of sins, Lord, who could stand?" (Psalm 130:3 NIV). Yet it is so easy to slip on to the judge's bench and point fingers. Let us leave the judging to God and become the best forgivers in the kingdom. After all, he forgave us.

Reflection

Have you ever experienced a crisis in forgiving?

_____

Describe how this was resolved.

_____

_____

What scripture verse(s) might encourage you to pursue forgiveness in a difficult circumstance?

_____

_____

_____

What do you think Jesus meant when he said, "Forgive us our sins, as we forgive those who sin against us?"

_____

_____

Write your own prayer of forgiveness:

_____

_____

_____

Father, pull us up short whenever we are tempted to withhold forgiveness from anyone. Love through us and forgive through us. Heal through us. Restore through us. For your kingdom's sake and for your glory. In Jesus's name. Amen.

JUDGING

For in the same way you judge others, you will be judged, and with the measure you use, it will be measured to you.

—Matthew 7:2 (NIV)

When we had the opportunity to hire Maria, we jumped at the chance. She is an astute businesswoman, having served as a senior vice president in an international business firm, and she is a dedicated woman of faith. As she took the helm of one of our ministries, her insights and strategic planning confirmed our decision.

Transitions can be difficult for any organization, and church groups are not exempt. I sat with Maria through many tense meetings, and she was the picture of grace and authority. In stressful situations, Maria was factual, always avoiding negativity.

But she was challenged when she traveled to South America for a conference. She arrived to a city known for its high crime rate. Wanting to reach her destination as quickly as possible, Maria grabbed a cab and issued directions. She noticed that the driver traveled a circuitous route and continued from the time he picked her up. Having lived in New York for years, Maria knew that cabbies often drive out of the way in order to hike rates. She stayed quiet but became rather annoyed.

Finally arriving at her destination, Maria learned that kidnappings occurred regularly in the city whenever drivers stop for red lights. Her savvy driver had been making a turn every time he saw a red light—to keep her safe.

In telling her story, Maria asked how often we make judgments of people based on prior experience or foolish suspicion. There was no basis for her false appraisal, one that would result in her safekeeping. Maria reminded us that Jesus told us not to judge (Matthew 7:1), and if we do, we'll be judged by the same measure. Do we look at fellow travelers with mercy and compassion, making allowances for background or circumstances?

A good thing to remember when we feel obliged to judge: there is always one more thing that we don't know about that person.

Reflection

Have you ever found yourself judging someone you don't know well?

_____

_____

Do you make a practice of judging people? _____ _____ ___ Have you ever found yourself wrong in your conclusions? If so, describe the incident:

_____

_____

I once heard someone say that judging is assigning motive to action. Using that guideline, how can we possibly know what someone is thinking when he is acting?

_____

_____

Have you ever been judged falsely? _____

If so, how did it feel?_____

What active measures can be taken to end the practice of judging?

_____

_____

Father, thank you for the grace that covers us. If you should mark iniquities, who would stand? We've all fallen short of your righteousness and constantly need your mercy. Help us, in turn, to be merciful. In Jesus's name. Amen.

MORE LITTLE THINGS

For God speaks in one way, and in two.

—Job 33:14 (ESV)

I am convinced that God communicates all the time; we just do not always have our receivers turned on or we do not attribute the message as coming from him.

Do you remember Tolstoy's story "Where Love Is, God Is,"[19] about Martin Avdeitch, who dreamed Jesus would appear to him the following day? The dream was so convincing that he awoke the next day in great anticipation. On that frosty morning, Martin saw Stepanich shoveling snow, invited him in for a warm drink, and told him about Jesus. Later, he saw a young woman with a baby shivering in the cold. He brought them into his cozy home, gave them warm clothes, food, and money, and told them about Jesus. Then he saw a boy stealing from an old lady. He settled their argument and gave love and compassion to them both. All day long Martin reached out in love preparing to see Jesus.

Evening came, and in the night Martin's heart was heavy. Although he had prepared, God had not visited him as expected. Martin grappled with disappointment, and one by one, the people he had helped appeared. There was Stepanich, the young woman and her baby, and the thief and his victim. That was when Martin realized God had indeed been present. He just hadn't recognized him in his varied forms.

Today would have been my mom's ninety-first birthday. Every time I visited her, she would quote Mother Julian of Norwich, saying, "All is well." As I think of Momo, I am in another city sharing about the loving ministries of missions. I have had a small matter of some urgency: I left my pajamas at home. My team and I made a side trip to the local Walmart where I found a set of nightclothes with writing all over them. It was not until I prepared for bed that I read the message: "All is well."

Momo, thank you for reminding me that our Father is everywhere present, and he still speaks.

Reflections

We don't have to be mystics to sit quietly awaiting God's voice. We can still ourselves while inviting him to be present and to speak. A good exercise to prepare our hearts is to take a passage of scripture and thoughtfully ponder its meaning and application to our lives. Ask, what is God saying to me in this verse? What is he revealing about himself? What is he asking me to do?

Thomas Merton, Christian writer and theologian, suggests eight attitudes that open us to God's presence: faith, openness, attention, reverence, expectation, supplication, trust, and joy. We can begin now to cultivate the practice of God's presence as we wait and listen.

Begin now to anticipate God's words. What gentle thoughts are struggling for expression? Be still and know

_____

_____

_____

Lord, open our ears, our eyes, and our hearts to receive you however you wish to make yourself known. In Jesus's name. Amen.

THE DREAM

I, the Lord, reveal myself to them in visions, I speak
to them in dreams.

—Numbers 12:6 (NIV)

God compassionately touched a friend during a time of extreme psychological and spiritual peril.

He was going through a rough patch, tougher than anything he had ever experienced. Not only was he physically exhausted, he felt emotionally and spiritually drained. His spiritual friends were encouraging him to wait for God's intervention. That was part of the problem. He'd been a devout believer since childhood but now was so depleted; there was no longer strength in him to hold on. He collapsed in a chair and closed his eyes.

As he drifted, he saw himself climbing a steep mountain. It seemed to be made of granite, and he knew if he stopped climbing, he would fall into the sheer chasm below. The more he climbed, the more the small reserve of strength ebbed from his weakened body. Finally, he reached a plateau that offered respite.

He reflected on how his friends and family had hailed him through the years as the strong, persistent leader who never quit, who never gave up. But here he was on the climb of his life, unable to see the mountain's peak yet knowing that stopping would be fatal.

In the middle of his painful reflections, he heard a thundering sound, and to his horror, he saw a great herd of Clydesdale horses stampeding across the highlands toward him. *This is the end,* he thought. *Perhaps this is the peace that I've been craving.* Still there was fear as the monstrous animals grew nearer with each second.

Finally, the leader of the herd galloped toward him and began lowering himself over his trembling body. *I'll be crushed*, he thought. And suddenly, he cried out, "Oh, Jesus."

The horse stopped abruptly and said, "What did you say?"

"Jesus," the man repeated.

"Oh, my precious Jesus," was the response. "Climb on my back, and I'll carry you over these mountains."

He awoke, knowing that he had been dreaming. Even so, he knew the dream was true, and he could trust God to make a way over the mountains.

Reflection

Think of all the times the Bible records God's messages given in dreams. Consider Joseph's cellmates and their prophetic dreams (Genesis 40), Pharaoh's dream (Genesis 41), Nebuchadnezzar and his great image (Daniel 2), Daniel and his prophetic dream of the world's kingdoms (Daniel 7), Joseph's dreams to go and return from Egypt (Matthew 2:13, 19), and others regarding the nature and use of dreams.

Why might God find it desirable to communicate in dreams?

_____

_____

Have you or any of your acquaintances experienced guidance or insight through dreams?

_____

_____

Father, I have watched my friend and learned that you provide whatever we need, no matter how difficult the circumstance. Cause us to glorify you in hard times by trusting you to make a way. In Jesus's name. Amen.

CONFOUNDED

For my thoughts are not your thoughts, neither are
your ways my ways, saith the Lord.

—Isaiah 55:8 (KJV)

I n my thoughts I am in company with the disciples as we walk
to Emmaus after the death of Jesus. The conversation is replete
with tears and disillusionment, downcast faces and dashed hopes.
We watched Jesus heal and do miracles. We even saw him bring the
dead back to life. But now it seems we must have missed something.
Some vital aspect of his teaching.

We trusted God. We had expectations, oh, yes, we had
expectations. We believed he would come to his throne (with us
beside him) in a certain way, just as the prophets had foretold.
Remembering how Jesus had delayed when he learned that his dear
friend Lazarus was ill and then performed the greatest miracle of all,
we were puzzled when Jesus didn't have another surprise up his sleeve
that would ultimately prove his claims as Son of God.

New Zealand missionary Joy Dawson once preached
spontaneously about the miracle of Lazarus's resurrection. She
recalled that the sisters Mary and Martha had expected Jesus to
arrive and heal Lazarus on the spot. Instead, Jesus disappointed
them by delaying his coming. After all, they were Jesus's special
friends and his frequent hosts when he needed to find a quiet place
of rest. One might think Jesus was indebted to this family. Instead,
the miracle that followed the initial disappointment far surpassed
the healing the sisters had desired. Dawson asked her audience, "Do
you want a healing or a resurrection?"

Without meditating on the magnitude of God's power, it would
seem that we are satisfied with Band-Aids rather than stepping

by faith into the possibilities of the divine in our daily lives. Our thimbles of faith are embarrassing when we remember that God is able to do more than we can ask or think (Ephesians 3:20). How often do we limit God's work by our minimal expectations?

Reflection

Have you ever been puzzled by God's response or seeming lack of response to your prayers? What did you do?

_____

_____

_____

_____

The doting grandmother of a little boy promised to buy him a special book for his birthday. His birthday came and passed, and still he heard nothing from his grandmother. Seeing his disappointment, the boy's mother suggested he write his grandmother a thank you note. Within days the boy received a card from his grandmother saying that she had not been able to find the book but was sending instead a check for him to buy what he wanted. She had not forgotten him and provided a gift to show she cared.

Could it be that in our relationship with our Father, all the gifts and signs of favor are not nearly as much as receiving the gift of his presence, of his "well done"?

Take time to write a thank you note to our heavenly Father, remembering even the small things that bring joy to our days.

_____

_____

_____

_____

Father, forgive me when my faith is earthbound. You are God. Let your will be done. In Jesus's name. Amen.

JUST ASK

You do not have because you do not ask God.
—James 4:2 (NIV)

W e were beyond exhausted after three hard weeks on Uganda's bumpy roads and multiple meetings. Finally reaching the airport, we learned there would be a fifteen-hour delay due to the plane's mechanical problems. We loaded ourselves back into the van for a return trip to the Namirembe Guest House.

Upon arrival, the two men on the team announced they would see what compensation the airlines could provide for causing us to miss our connections in London and Detroit. Naively, as the newbie on the team, I asked if they would bump us up to better seats for our eighteen-plus-hour flights. The heads of my companions pivoted, and they laughed as if I'd asked for a private jet to take us home.

I was determined. "Ye have not, because ye ask not" (James 4:2 KJV), I reminded the team.

An hour later, the fellows returned, and I asked—expectantly, "Did we get bumped up?"

With gentle laughter, the response was negative, but we were to be treated to lunch in a London hotel and given our own day rooms. Of course, that was lovely, and I was grateful, but it was not what I had hoped.

The familiar food in London and a hot shower with a nap were delightful. A vehicle delivered us back to the airport, and we were escorted to our point of departure. Since our connections had been disrupted, our team was seated in various places throughout the coach section. I sat with a team member, buckled up, and prepared for the next leg of the trip.

I turned on my inflight entertainment screen, but nothing happened. My companion also tried, unsuccessfully, to work my screen. Then the steward did his best to make the apparatus work.

"Just wait until we're airborne," he assured me, "and I'll reboot this from the controls."

However, many miles later and after many buttons were pushed unsuccessfully, the steward asked if I minded being relocated.

"No, but I have to bring my friend," I replied.

"Of course," he said.

A short time later, he reappeared. "I've looked all over the economy seating and can't find a vacant seat. Would you mind if I put you in business class?"

"Of course not," I answered with a huge smile.

In minutes we were ushered down the aisle. Gratefully, I was reminded, "You have not for you ask not." "Ask, and you will receive" (Matthew 7:7 Contemporary English Version). It's a lesson I haven't forgotten.

Reflection

Should knowing God's love for us give us courage to present our requests to him?

_____

_____

_____

Read Elijah's experience in 1 Kings 19 after he ran away from Jezebel's army. What did the angel say to him?

_____

_____

_____

What does this reveal about God's care for his children?

_____

_____

_____

Why might God have answered my prayer when there are so many other more weighty needs that seem to go unanswered?

_____

_____

_____

Lord, I wonder how many blessings, large and small, we miss because we're afraid to ask. Help us remember that you're a good Father who loves to give good gifts to your undeserving children, and we honor you by asking. Thank you again. Amen.

SWEET JOSEPHINE

But ask the animals, and they will teach you ...
that the hand of the Lord has done this? In his
hand is the life of every creature and the breath of
all mankind.

—Job 12:7, 9–10 (NIV)

Today I came across a picture of Josephine. It evoked nostalgia and reminded me of the bond we formed in months of working in Kampala, the capital of Uganda.

The night was rainy, one of those times when the skies seem to be falling and the raindrops sting when they hit you. In the middle of that thunderous monsoon, I heard a sound of desperate crying coming from somewhere near. I wanted to pretend I hadn't heard that piercing wail and tried to go back to sleep. But the moans wouldn't stop.

Finally, I put on my robe, picked up my umbrella and flashlight, and headed out the door. Louder and louder the cries came as I approached the huge rubbish pit just below my terrace. I shined the light all around the bottom of the hole, and about fourteen feet down, I saw a terrified dog who had fallen in during her nightly forage for food. I called to her, but there was nothing I could do until the household woke up and I could get a ladder.

Several hours later, when the house lights came on, Gilbert and Jackson put on their rain slickers, got a ladder, and followed me. The three of us were eventually able to get the frightened animal out of the hole.

Josephine (so named because we had pulled her out of the pit) became my constant companion during that lonely stint in Kampala.

Whenever I needed a little reminder of home, Josephine was there. And she shared that same unconditional love with all our visitors.

Finally, the day came for me to pack up and begin my eighteen hour plus trip home. I couldn't bear to tell Josephine I was leaving, but somehow she knew and haunted my doorway all day long. Then she disappeared. When the driver appeared to take me to the airport that night, I saw a movement in the bushes. It was Josephine. She had come out to say goodbye. And then she was gone.

Is it wishful thinking to believe God had sent her just to bring me companionship at a lonely time? That she stayed to demonstrate unconditional love to the other family members in the compound and that Josephine changed a tiny piece of culture?

Reflection

I'm an animal lover, and in intervals of visiting with other cultures, I have learned a new appreciation for all God's creation, including the animals. A wonderful and amusing Bible story has a rebellious prophet arguing with a donkey. Read it for yourself (Numbers 22:21–39). Balaam is disregarding God's order in dealing with pagan King Balak. Only the faithful donkey saves him.

Have you ever thought of animals as ministering spirits? Describe such an experience:

_____

_____

_____

_____

Do you think God has a role for animals in this world? If so, what?

_____

_____

_____

Note any references to animals in the Bible that indicate God's care and concern for them:

_____

_____

_____

_____

Father, I am so grateful for the demonstrations of love you shower on us. Thank you especially for sweet Josephine, wonderful blessing, from you who created all things. Amen.

TRUST

Trust in the Lord with all your heart and lean not
on your own understanding.

—Proverbs 3:5 (NIV)

L ife can be fraught with the unexpected, particularly in mission
work. One of our long-term missionaries says that being flexible
is insufficient; one must be fluid.

A reminder of God's constant provision awaited me at our
annual church council meeting. I had been asked to read the very
long passage in John about Jesus's meeting the woman at the well.
After I reached the podium, all the house lights were extinguished
save for blinding spotlights that were aimed my way. Slowly, I
read John 4:4–42. At the end of the reading, the spotlights were
immediately dimmed, leaving the hall in complete darkness—and
my eyes temporarily unseeing as a result of the powerful spotlights.

Immediately, horrific thoughts ran through my mind. *Oh, God,
how am I getting out of here?* was my immediate quandary. Calculating
the distance between where I stood and the drop-off leading to the
next level, I began sliding my feet inches at a time. Meanwhile, the
actress on the other side of the stage began dramatizing the Samaritan
woman's story. No one seemed aware of my frightening predicament.

Cautiously, I continued inching toward the dropoff: *What if I
crash and fall? What if the whole service is disrupted by the noise?* As I
edged closer to that treacherous step, a hand reached out to me in
the darkness and quietly guided me to safety. Santos had seen my
dilemma and was there waiting to rescue me. I couldn't see his face,
but I felt his strong grip, and I sensed his reassuring smile.

Just like Jesus—seeing the danger that lay just ahead of me and
putting himself at the place of need to save me and to keep me from
falling—my friend was there.

Reflection

Isn't it interesting that so often the first message angels speak is, "Fear not." We live in the unknown and the unexpected, and it's imperative that we have confidence that God holds our present and our future in his hand.

Trust is built through relationship. We don't trust someone we don't know. As we continue our faith journey with Christ, he creates opportunities for trusting. We find ourselves in quandaries with no resolutions. There are unimagined challenges. Our finest studies never showed us how to unravel some of the tangles that imperil even ordinary days. And so, we live in the middle of managed chaos— until we consciously decide to cast our cares on him. We start to believe that he really might care for us.

When we begin practicing his presence, handing our cares to him and launching every concern on the possibility that Jesus is who and what he says he is, that literary image becomes reality. What we've read becomes truth, and hope becomes fact.

Have you ever had a glimpse of Jesus and knew he was Lord?

_____

_____

Or have you seen Jesus living through another person?

_____

_____

Describe the situation:

_____

_____

Have you continued to trust Jesus?

_____

_____

Father, continue to strengthen my faith and teach me to trust. You said you "[are] able to keep [us] from stumbling and to present [us] before [your] glorious presence without fault and with great joy" (Jude 1:24 NIV). Your promise is enough. Amen.

GOD KNOWS

The Lord giveth wisdom: out of his mouth cometh
knowledge and understanding.
—Proverbs 2:6 (KJV)

Any amalgam of figures beyond basic sums and arithmetic has
always been challenging to me. When my counselor told me
that in order to receive my diploma for a postgraduate degree, the
final course I needed to take was advanced multivariate statistics, I
almost froze in horror.

I protested long and hard: "This is supposed to be the easiest
class I have to take. It's my last," I complained. He had guided me so
deftly for years, and here at the end he was putting my GPA in peril.

I would like to say Dr. Grey was sympathetic, but instead, I
think he rather enjoyed my plight. He tried to ease my discomfort by
saying the professor was someone everybody loved and that I would
have no trouble. (But somewhere behind all the protest, I think a
smile lurked.) I left his office wondering how I would ever make it
through that final course while continuing with my missions work.

I arrived early the first day of class in order to visit with the
professor that "everybody loved" only to discover that her class load
hadn't permitted her to teach the course. Instead, I was confronted
with a very young man wearing hiking shorts and boots and who
was new to the faculty—someone who, obviously, had to prove
himself. I really was between what we in Texas call a rock and a
hard place.

After the first class, with material that seemed vaguely familiar,
I took my text home and began studying. *And praying.* Every page
was read and reread and prayed over. God had created systems and
numbers and ways of interpreting data, so I went straight to the

Source. And I went next to Matt. (That's what our new professor told us to call him. Not Dr. Matt … just Matt.) Every time he had office hours, I was there learning from him. And I prayed.

Advanced multivariate statistics is not the only challenge I've had, but I learned through that and other similar lessons that I don't have to lean on my own understanding when I'm in God's will—that *he* gives knowledge and understanding, being all-knowing and the creator of all things. We do our part (studying, in this case), and he gives us everything we need to follow him and to do his will. We must never allow circumstances to defeat us. He either provides the way through or gives us the resources to resolve them or the grace to live in them.

In everything, we are more than conquerors through Christ Jesus. *I am not a mathematician*, but I finished that class with an A. Yea, God.

Reflection

Personally speaking, I'm glad God doesn't limit his concerns to liturgy, sacraments, and altar hangings. So much of our lives is spent outside the four walls of our church buildings and inside the confines of our minds. While the community sees, if it takes time to notice, our daily activities, only God really knows about the cares in our hearts.

What do you do when your circle of responsibility outranks the realm of your understanding? After you've consulted the specialists in your life, where do you turn?

I find God's conversation with Job—after that convoluted discussion between Job and his friends—somewhat amusing.

God: "Who came up with the blueprints and measurements [of the earth]?

Job: silence.

God: "Have you ever ordered morning, 'Get up!' told Dawn, 'Get to work!'?"

Job: silence.

God: "Do you know the first thing about death?"

Job: silence.

God: "Do you have any idea how large this earth is?"

Job: silence (Job 38:5, 12, 17–18 MSG).

Musing on God's infinite knowledge, why should we ever limit him to the small world of our understanding? When we need help, why not ask God?

Have you ever asked God's help in areas outside the realm of the spiritual? What happened?

_____

_____

_____

Read Job 40–42 to expand your thinking about our amazing Father.

Father, thank you that you care about all our cares, even those that seem trivial to everyone else. Strengthen our faith to trust you in all things and to stand still to see your salvation. In Jesus's name. Amen.

A QUIET TIME

Be still and know that I am God.
—Psalm 46:10 (KJV)

There are tiny spaces throughout our calendars that permit moments, sometimes days, for inactivity. We call those holidays, such as Christmas and New Year's Day. Without feeling guilty, we can take advantage of those special times. Otherwise, our frenetic lifestyles demand that every slot be filled, robbing us of the quiet in which our souls are nourished.

A story is told of an early explorer who was trekking across the jungles in the interior of Africa. Preparation had been made for the rigors of a dangerous and difficult journey. The explorer had been advised about the significant differences between the Western concept of time and African time, and he had been cautioned to honor the daily plans of the head porter.

Initially, the traveler was content to follow his men, who spent arduous hours hacking through vines and skirting swamps in search of their destination. Finally, however, he grew tired of making such slow progress and determined that they could make better time. In spite of being told that his success would depend on going only a certain distance each day, he ordered the lead porter to plan on going further the following day.

At midmorning, the men began grumbling. The path seemed to become more hazardous. Here and there, men needed breaks for water. Instead of the companionable chattering that ran up and down the line, there was now an undercurrent of irritation. When it was time to set up camp, there were no songs.

The next morning, the explorer awakened to silence. There was no movement in the camp. As he went from tent to tent, he saw that no one was stirring. Finding his head porter, the man wondered what was happening with the porters. Sensing his frustration, the porter explained that they had traveled so fast during the previous day that they were waiting for their souls to catch up.

We are given the precious gift of time, and it is a gift given equally to us all. It is time to let our souls catch up, acknowledge God, bask in his love, and nourish our relationship with him. It is time to be still, to know, and to heed his voice.

Reflection

My university advisor was a time-management consultant. Throughout his classes, we had the opportunity to learn many of the concepts he taught corporate leaders. One of the first things he told us is that time cannot be managed. It is. No one person has more time than another, and no one person has less than another. We all have the same amount of time. What we must learn to do, according to my advisor, is manage ourselves regarding time.

I've read that Martin Luther said he had so much to do that he couldn't get on without spending three hours in prayer. And John Wesley apparently spent two hours praying each day. Others write about the need to pray or meditate or study God's Word throughout the day. How, I wonder, were they able to find the time to pray or study when they had so much to do? Perhaps, using my advisor's language, they learned to manage themselves regarding time.

If you were to reorder your priorities, what would your daily schedule look like?

_____

_____

_____

If you don't yet have a time for daily prayer, where might you carve a spot for prayer and fellowship with God? (It doesn't have to be a long time, but you may find that you enjoy those moments so dearly that they grow incrementally.)

_____

_____

Rewrite this verse in your own words: "Be still and know that I am God."

_____

_____

Father, the world is too much with us. There are so many distractions. Thank you for time to reorder ourselves and our priorities. Amen.

QUESTIONING

A person's steps are directed by the Lord. How then
can anyone understand their own way?
—Proverbs 20:24 (NIV)

H ave you ever wondered if an opportunity for service is actually
God's call or if it's just another slot that needs to be filled?
When we received an unusual invitation, we asked for confirmation
that this was something we were to do.

We had been asked to conduct a retreat for a group of missionaries
in a tropical land. This is a somewhat atypical mission experience.
We usually go to build buildings, stage VBS, treat sick animals,
pull bad teeth, teach people how to keep their water safe, and those
kinds of things. And we do conduct conferences, but they are for
local partners, not for the missionaries. This time we were asked to
provide spiritual refreshment for the doers themselves.

In addition to weeks of team meetings and gathering supplies and
appropriate clothing, we bought our tickets and made appointments
for immunizations. All the while we prayed and wondered about
the missionaries to whom we would be ministering. We learned
that the group was from varying Christian traditions, and all had
different ministries. How would we possibly plan a retreat that spoke
to each one?

Prayer was the central focus of our preparations. We asked for
wisdom and discernment, and we cobbled together an agenda that
we sensed God had given us. Then we prayed some more.

On opening day, we asked the mission directors to lead us each
day with a devotional time. As we listened and prayed (again), the
first leader began with the *exact theme we had chosen.* The next day
the same thing occurred. We had brought books as gifts for each day,

and it just happened that the devotionals given by the missionary leaders were taken from the books we had brought as gifts.

Even coming from different traditions and practices, God's love through his Spirit shined through, and we were one.

Reflection

I heard a rather curious and quaint story about a woman who was seeking God's direction about a decision. Perhaps this comes under the heading of broom closet scripture, but I share it because of the trusting heart that it reveals.

The woman was entrusted by her brothers with the oversight of their mother's care. The three siblings had determined that there would be no medically induced extension of life interventions in the event of an end-of-life occurrence. When, after the course of time, the doctors recommended a blood transfusion, the daughter agreed.

Later, however, she was guilt-ridden thinking she had violated her brothers' wishes. She began praying, relinquishing her mother to God and asking that he would mercifully overrule any wrong actions on her part. In spite of all the additional medical attention her mother received, she died peacefully surrounded by those she loved.

Look at these verses:

- "I will instruct you and teach you in the way you should go; I will guide you with my eye" (Psalm 32:8 NKJV).
- "Whether you turn to the right or to the left, your ears will hear a voice behind you, saying, 'This is the way; walk in it'" (Isaiah 30:21 NIV).
- "Teach me the way in which I should walk; for to you I lift up my soul" (Psalm 143:8 NASB).
- "In all thy ways acknowledge him, and he shall direct thy paths" (Proverbs 3:6 KJV).

Do you rely on any of these scriptures as you prayerfully seek God's direction?

_____

_____

Are there other verses that inform your prayers for guidance?

_____

_____

How do you seek confirmation for direction?

_____

_____

Father, strengthen our trust in your guidance, and help us to obey, trusting your faithfulness. In Jesus's name. Amen.

FELLOW TRAVELERS

4

FELLOW TRAVELERS

The journey may sometimes be lonely but, often as not, it
is frequented with those whose quest incites our longing
for more than we've yet discovered. There are those who,
like Moses, count it a joy to suffer for Jesus, or Aidan,
who journeyed as a servant among his people.
How can we learn from those who walk with us? What
characteristics will help us access the wisdom of fellow travelers?

LOST AND FOUND

But thanks be to God, who gives us the victory
through our Lord Jesus Christ.
                    —1 Corinthians 15:57 (KJV)

One of our missioners shared a story about a time after the death
of her mother when mission "brought her home." She was a
teen who had drifted away from her church family and was confused
and angry. The mission trip became available, and the young lady's
father told her she was going. Although she had mixed feelings, Dad
held firm, and off she went with the team, three shovels, garden
gloves, and no idea what was ahead.

The team headed south, crossed into Mexico, and stopped in
Monterrey to paint a church. Next, they went to Camp Hayah in
the countryside where they lodged in buildings with bunk beds but
no mattresses, no electricity, and no running water. Their assignment
was to dig a foundation for a new building with the three shovels
and two pickaxes they had brought. And the gloves would come in
handy.

After several days of backbreaking work, they had made almost
no progress. But the sugary Mexican Cokes were delicious, and the
Christian fellowship was a welcomed return to the life the teen had
known with her parents. As her personal foundation emerged, the
work came to an abrupt halt when most of the team was assailed
with "Montezuma's revenge" (a colloquial term for travelers' diarrhea
contracted in Mexico).

They lay on their bare bunks sipping Cokes and sweating. And
then they heard it: a large commercial vehicle pulled up and started
shoveling tons of dirt from the squared-off area that had been
assaulted by a team of teenagers hoping to dig a hole for the new

foundation. In two hours the machine finished the job, and with blistered hands, swirling stomachs, and sunburned faces, the team was so grateful.

When all was said and done, the young woman who thought she was going to help others found that she had rediscovered her spiritual home. God took her offering and blessed her with healing and unconditional love. She left part of herself at Camp Hayah but returned home with part of that place in her heart knowing she had reclaimed her roots and her Christian family.

Reflection

I once heard someone say, "When God seems far away, guess who moved?" What are some of the reasons we may feel distanced from God?

_____

_____

Write down the passage from 2 Corinthians 5:7.

_____

_____

How can this verse keep us spiritually on track?

_____

_____

Father, as in the story of the Prodigal son, you are so precious to watch and wait for our return when we slip away from you. Draw our hearts always and evermore to you. In Jesus's name. Amen.

ABOUNDING JOY

Whether we live, we live unto the Lord; and whether we die, we die unto the Lord: whether we live therefore, or die, we are the Lord's.

—Romans 14:8 (KJV)

I recently returned from a marriage and ministry conference that we conducted for pastors and their wives in northern Kenya. Having worked with this group in the past, I looked forward to renewing acquaintances.

Sure enough, Moses was there. I first met him years ago as he was returning from an evangelistic outreach. I had heard about the persecution he and his friends had experienced. To my astonishment, Moses and the team were laughing and actually happy that they had been counted worthy to be shot at and to suffer for Jesus, just as the early Church rejoiced in their hardships. Remembering our last encounter, I asked Moses if he'd had the bullets removed from his leg. With a big smile, he said they were too close to some nerves to risk removal.

Then I met Matthew, one of the praise musicians who hails from another African country. When he was a security officer, he had been ordered to shoot peaceful protesters but refused. In retaliation, government officers shot Matthew in the head, and he lost sight in one eye but was recovering when he was warned that some men were en route to the hospital to finish him off. Meanwhile, the military went to Matthew's house and killed his wife. Matthew escaped and took three of his children with him to Kenya. Since coming to Kenya, his country's government has kidnapped two of the children, but Matthew continues to praise and trust God.

My friend Toch, director of the ministry, has been stoned and ambushed numbers of times—three times the pistol placed to his head didn't fire. Toch lives to talk about Jesus and to witness to his saving grace. He and his band of merry disciples work throughout the north of Kenya, bringing hope where there is despair and demonstrating Christ's love and life through their words and deeds.

I see the Church when I am with these Christian brothers and sisters—joyous and counting each day precious. They understand the kingdom of God and life in the kingdom. I watch former members of warring tribes embrace and support one another when they begin to acknowledge the same Father. I follow these disciples into slum areas to share food and Bible stories with prostitutes as they walk together, bringing hope and new life.

I stand respectfully listening to their stories and am humbled that they invite me to participate in their lives. While our circumstances may be different, we are children of the same Father having different mothers.

Reflection

I was about twelve years old when I heard a missionary talk about living and working in Africa. His stories were fascinating. I went home thinking and wondering whether God was calling me to leave everything and become a missionary to Africa.

The thought tormented me throughout Sunday afternoon. As a child, I was consumed with the fear that I would have to leave my family and friends forever to be in Africa. There was no joy; just a fearsome *thou shalt*. I finally told God I was willing to go, and the compelling demand left.

Decades later, when the call was clear, there was assurance and peace. I am learning that even with the most difficult of tasks, God's call is always accompanied by his peace. When I initially met my Kenyan friends, my first impression was their abounding joy. As I continue the relationship, I see that walking with Jesus is always "fullness of joy" and devoid of fear and trepidation.

Why do you think we are sometimes fearful of doing God's will?

_____

_____

Looking at Toch's merry band from Kenya, how would you explain their joy?

_____

_____

Memorize this verse: "In this world you will have trouble. But take heart! I have overcome the world" (John 16:33 NIV).

Father, be with my Kenyan friends who count their lives as nothing for the sake of the Gospel. Keep them safe as they go. Keep me faithful in my circumstances knowing that I too bear your name. In Jesus's name. Amen.

OUT OF NOWHERE

For whosoever shall do the will of God, the same is
my brother, and my sister, and mother.

—Mark 3:35 (KJV)

This wonderful story came from my dear rector reflecting on his
first mission to Africa:

Out of nowhere came the blackest man I'd ever seen, and he was
walking toward me with his unnaturally long arms outstretched like
a raptor to consume me, his crooked white teeth as bright as keys on
a Steinway. He enveloped me in his arms, and I became untethered
from the pain I had carried like a backpack the 8,861 miles from
San Antonio to Kenya.

I rested there, indifferent to the time, until he took me by the
shoulders and said, "Patrick, we are brothers, you and I, because our
mother [singular] told us to forgive."

I was beyond exhaustion when John, my newly found South
Sudanese brother, embraced me. By that time, Kay and I had been
traveling for fifty-seven hours straight. We had finally arrived in
Marsabit, Kenya, at the crossroads of Ethiopia, Uganda, South
Sudan, and Somalia, and situated among fifteen ancient tribes who
exist there in an uneasy peace. In fact, on the night we arrived,
twelve men were murdered in a tribal feud over the theft of cows,
the gold of that region.

Four months before the coronavirus would monopolize our lives,
Kay and I were asked to speak at a Pastors and Wives Conference for
clergy families living in that isolated region. I did not think many
would make it. The report of the murders, just two miles from the
Catholic Center where we were holding the conference, dominated
the news. At the same time, the road up to the center was a tower

of chocolate mud two feet deep. I walked into the hall that first morning to see that every one of the thirty couples was present and dressed in matching colorful outfits without a speck of mud, dirt, or dust on them. Knowing they all lived in thatched-roof homes along isolated, rutted roads, they seemed to have appeared *out of nowhere.*

The people's humility and honesty undressed my Western pretension. Here, at the top of this muddy, rutted, nearly impassable promontory, encircled by enemies of the cross, were people who loved Jesus more than breath. And then of all things, John wrapped his arms around me. I shuddered in my own moment of repentance.

John, for his part, grew up in a village in South Sudan. The youngest of six, he is part of one of the oldest clans of Christians on earth. Tragedy struck when his father died when John was but one month old. Without warning, his uncles, his father's brothers, descended on their home and took all their cows. In short order, the family of seven found themselves in a sprawling refugee camp, living in a house of tin and cardboard, from which there seemed no exit.

And then, one day, in that forlorn place, his mother took John aside and seemingly *out of nowhere*, said, "Forgive your uncles, or it will eat you from the inside out."

Hearing the story of my violent childhood household and my mother's identical prescription, John determined we were brothers. Not blood, but forgiveness and grace bound us together.

Reflection

Patrick's story suggests that he was surprised at every turn of his Kenyan mission—the warmth, the devotion, the appearances, the commitment. What was the common ingredient that bound everyone together?

_____

_____

Do you ever make snap judgments about people or situations?

_____

_____

_____

What have you learned from these experiences?

_____

_____

_____

Is there a difference between judging and discerning?

_____

_____

What does Scripture say about judging?

_____

_____

About discerning?

_____

_____

Thank you, Father, that you continue to teach us with your lovely surprises. Amen.

THE SONG

Singing psalms and hymns and spiritual songs among yourselves, and making music to the Lord in your hearts.

—Ephesians 5:19 (New Living Translation)

We noticed him immediately—front teeth missing, with a toddler cradled in his lanky arms. He had quietly stood in line for his breakfast taco, beans, and pineapple and respectfully participated in communion. Then suddenly, the margins at the Mexican border were filled with his clear and melodic voice. It wasn't just a brief little ditty. He sang on and on with bursts of staccato phrasing—obviously a canticle of praise. And we were moved beyond that border feeding station.

Wagons of food had been filled and pulled across the concrete link that was the gateway to dreams for which so many risked their lives. We knew people would be waiting for the breakfast that would sustain them until the next act of kindness would be proffered. As I pulled my wagon, I anticipated a scene of chaos, disorder, grasping from the ragtag I thought would be awaiting us.

Instead, we were greeted warmly, and lines quietly and patiently formed in front of us as we set up our makeshift cafeteria. One by one, Cubans, Hondurans, Guatemalans, and others took their plates with, "Gracias," "*Dios la bendiga*" (God bless you), or heavily accented, "Thank you." No pushing, no grabbing, just quiet gratitude.

Two clergy set up communion for everyone who wanted to remember our Lord's sacrifice. Drawn together from many places and many experiences, we shared Jesus as we worshipped. And that is when he broke out in song, a song that clearly recognized Jesus and our fellowship as we praised God together. The song transcended the suffering, setbacks, and disappointments that must have been felt. The song proclaimed the love of Christ in the middle of a broken world and would, ultimately, heal that world.

Reflection

Jesus was a refugee. As a toddler, his parents had to flee the same sort of terror many refugees seeking our southern border are trying to escape. Is that why the Old Testament staunchly commands that we love the foreigners living among us (Leviticus 19:34), providing justice for them (Deuteronomy 27:19; Zechariah 7:9–10; Exodus 12:49), and leaving food for them (Leviticus)? The New Testament clearly instructs us to love and care for everyone as brothers and sisters.

Politics aside, how can each of us be an expression of Jesus in ministering to the aliens among us?

_____

_____

_____

Do you remember what happened when Jesus took time to speak with the woman at the well? A woman marginalized by her own people? What resulted from this encounter?

_____

_____

Other stories in this collection remind us that God uses and multiplies all our efforts to share his love. We may not see the harvest in our lifetime, but as we plant seeds, others will water, and God promises to give the increase (1 Corinthians 3:6–9).

Dear Lord, what a joy it is to witness your songs in the most unexpected places. We are grateful. Amen.

JESUS LOVES YOU

We love him because he first loved us.
—1 John 4:19 (KJV)

Joseph lives in an African country and is a convert to Christianity. His story is instructive.

Joseph was a well-known religious leader who was skilled in debate and an articulate speaker. One day two Christians appeared at his door. His sister answered, and they told her their business, which baffled her. She rushed to the salon where Joseph was seated and said, "There are two Christians here, and they want to talk to you."

Initially, Joseph refused to see them, but on a mischievous whim, he told his sister to show them to the salon. He knew he could decimate them with his words. Two very shy Christians stepped boldly into the lion's den, into Joseph's salon.

After Joseph welcomed them, one of the two men said, "We just came to tell you that Jesus loves you."

Joseph was taken aback. Everyone knew of him and his militant faith. How did these Christians dare come tell him about Jesus? Then Joseph asked the young men theological questions, to which their only response was, "We don't know. We only came to tell you that Jesus loves you."

Repeatedly, Joseph barraged them with words. They could only repeat their original statement, "We came to tell you that Jesus loves you." The men finally left, probably feeling completely dejected.

However, the story doesn't end there. Joseph couldn't stop thinking of those low-status, ignorant Christians who dared come to his door to tell him that Jesus loved him. He began to wonder, *Have I ever talked to anyone about my faith?* Joseph began a search to discover what it was that gave his visitors confidence and courage to speak about Jesus.

Initially, Joseph's research led him to non-Christian material that gave assent to Jesus's divine status. Then he was drawn to reading the Bible.

One day he said, "I am a Christian."

From that point on, he consumed the Bible and pursued fellowship in a local Christian church. Today he is a powerful Christian evangelist because two young men boldly shared God's love. Two young men who probably left Joseph's house thinking they had failed their Lord. Wondering why they had ever thought they might make a difference. Yet not only was Joseph's life transformed, the hundreds of people he reaches continue to be moved by the witness of two shy believers.

Let's pray to be one of them too.

Reflection

In a broken world, perhaps the most potent antidote we can give is Jesus's love. Think of how powerfully the manifestation of love transforms lives. Shy wallflowers become models of confidence when loved. Emotionally stressed people are made whole with love. Broken hearts are healed with love. We experience a bit of heaven on earth when we are touched by God's love.

Interestingly, God uses only one word to describe himself: love (1 John 4:8). No wonder Joseph was roused when he heard that Jesus loves him. In his world, where ritual and tradition were dominant, the thought of being loved by Jesus was overwhelming.

How do you recognize God's love in your life?

_____

_____

_____

_____

_____

How do you demonstrate God's love?

_____

_____

_____

_____

_____

Father, thank you for the people who speak your love to us. Make us bold to share your love and your Good News with those in our world. In Jesus's name. Amen.

FINDING GRACE

But he said to me, "My grace is sufficient for you,
for my power is made perfect in weakness."
—2 Corinthians 12:9 (NIV)

When my blonde friend Betty agreed to go to a Latin American country for a mission project, she did not hesitate. It didn't matter that she knew limited Spanish or that she'd never traveled to that part of the world. She had a willing heart.

Betty was told to go to a certain place, and there she would learn where to proceed. She bought her ticket, boarded the plane, and took a taxi to the regional bishop's office for further directions. She left believing that the next day the bishop's secretary would drive her to her destination.

The following morning, Betty returned to the bishop's office, and instead of taking her to the project, the secretary took her to the bus station, handed her a ticket for the next leg of the journey, and assured her that her coworker, a tall red-haired woman, would meet her. Then she left.

Betty made her way through the long line of waiting people. She climbed on to the bus and looked around for a seat. As she peered through the rows of passengers already seated, she saw a wiry little man vigorously waving at her from the back of the bus. He called out, "Señora, señora," indicating he had a seat for her.

Betty moved to the rear of the bus and gratefully sat. She and her new friend began communicating with their few words of Spanish and English and generous waving of hands and arms. They compared tickets.

"Oh, no." She sighed. It looked like he would be getting off in another place at an earlier time.

Through the hot, dusty hours, Betty and her new friend talked, until, at a certain stop, he leaned over to say goodbye. Even though she'd only known him a short while, Betty suddenly felt bereft. She watched him go down the aisle and out the door. She turned her head to avoid seeing him walk away and looked back to see that he was returning. He had come back to see her to her destination.

Hours later, they reached the place where Betty was to meet her contact. The bus emptied, and the little man led Betty through the advancing crowds who were looking for loved ones.

Suddenly, the mass opened, and a tall, redheaded woman walked toward them with open arms. "You must be Betty," she said. And as they embraced, she said, "I'm Grace."

Betty turned to introduce Grace to her friend, but he was nowhere to be found. Instead, she had found Grace.

Reflection

Recall a time when you were surprised by grace.

_____

_____

_____

Scripture often reminds us that faith in Jesus empowers us to fulfill his commands. Jesus tells us that his commands are not difficult to obey (1 John 5:3). Look in Hebrews 11 for a common thread. How could this help in doing God's will?

_____

_____

_____

Father, your angels are ministering spirits who help us on our way, and we are constantly accompanied by your grace. Thank you that you give us everything we need to serve you faithfully. Amen.

SERVANTS

[Jesus] made himself of no reputation, and took
upon him the form of a servant, and was made in
the likeness of men: And being found in fashion as
a man, he humbled himself.

—Philippians 2:7–8 (KJV)

Aidan, the beloved saint who founded the Christian community
on the island of Lindisfarne in the seventh century, was known
to live and instruct his monks in the way of service. The devout
community that lived together divided their time between prayers,
study, work, and loving action for others. Aidan "learned to travel
lightly, knowing that the less you had the less you need fear being
robbed. The more you carried about with you, the more anxious and
burdened you became."[20]

Aidan taught his monks to walk among the people, not to ride
on horseback where they would be far above them and unable to talk
with them. Once the king handpicked a beautiful horse, equipped
it with a jewel-studded saddle and tack, and presented it to Aidan.
With heavy heart but gratitude for the king's generosity, Aidan left
the palace. He became anxious about robbers, about protecting his
valuable new possessions, and about being so high above his people.

Soon, he saw a beggar standing by the roadside and thought of
giving him the valuable saddle, and then it occurred to him that
the man would be unable to carry it. Immediately, he resolved his
dilemma by getting off the horse and handing it over along with
the saddle and tack, telling the beggar where it could be sold for a
good price.

Occasionally, we hear of contemporaries who have given
themselves in service for others. Think of Agnes Gonxha Bojaxhiu,

whom we know as Mother Theresa, a young woman from an affluent family who gave her life to serve lepers, the disabled, the blind, and the aged. What about Bill Bright, founder of Campus Crusade, who was discovered early one morning polishing all the shoes that had been left in the hall by the Korean staff? And there are so many others who gave themselves by serving others.

It's easy to talk and read of service, but the doing requires an inner relinquishment of pride, place, possession, time, and self. Where do we begin? Alternatively, how do we continue? Imagine the joy of sharing the company of these great men and women of God as we choose to follow Jesus in serving, sharing, and giving.

Reflection

Think of Jesus at the last supper. Knowing he would be humiliated, tortured, and killed within hours, the last thing he did for his disciples was wash their feet—those dusty, dirty feet that had touched the filth of the streets of Jerusalem.

What would it have been like to wash Peter's feet, knowing he would soon betray his Master? Think of washing the thief and betrayer Judas's feet. Thomas, the doubter, would be in the crowd. But Jesus, knowing who he was, had already emptied himself and assumed the nature of a servant.

Dietrich Bonhoeffer, in his *Letter and Papers from Prison*,[21] says adopting spiritual disciplines prior to severe testing enables one to stand up under the test. Jesus already practiced prayer and meditation, obedience and humility long before the agony at the Garden. Though a king, he had taken upon himself the heart of a servant.

What aspects of servanthood do you see in yourself?

_____

_____

_____

What servant traits would you like to acquire?

_____

_____

_____

For a reminder of Jesus's servant heart, read Isaiah 53.

Father, as people of the cross, make us doers as well as hearers of your Word. Show us now the door that opens to us in service. In Jesus's name. Amen.

PECULIAR

But ye are a chosen generation, a royal priesthood,
an holy nation, a peculiar people; that ye should
shew forth the praises of him who hath called you
out of darkness into his marvelous light.

—1 Peter 2:9 (KJV)

One of our partners from Uganda, named Sunday, came to
visit and talk about ministry at our churches. Sunday is the
director of the Women's Centre in northwest Nebbi and the national
facilitator of a microenterprise ministry for women called Threads
of Blessing. She came to spend three weeks with us and got here in
time to be quarantined out of her own country. She stayed with us
five months.

Sunday is one of those "peculiar" Christians. Instead of whining
about being stranded and worrying about the three small children
she left at home with relatives, she patiently trusted God to use her
for his purposes. She quietly made visits to mission supporters, made
videos about her work, and spent weekends working with our local
feeding program. When asked about being stuck here all this time,
Sunday flashed her broad smile and said, "It's okay." She didn't talk
about the solitary moments when she wept for her children and
home because Sunday trusts God with her family and her time. She
is odd measured by our hedonistic culture.

Growing up, we often heard sermons that reminded us that, as
Christians, we were to be peculiar, not conformed to self-orientation
but to God and thoughts of others. (Even now that call to being
peculiar makes me uncomfortable. I wonder if it's because I so want
to fit in?) In my childish mind, I was certain that *peculiar* referred to
the list of *thou shalt nots* that we read about in the Bible. For certain,

we weren't ascetics, but we did want to be faithful to follow Jesus. Maybe that was peculiar.

To my unsophisticated thinking, those differences could be summed up in a list of activities that could spill over into social behaviors and, if not careful, into judging. It has taken years for me to understand what Peter really meant when he described followers of Jesus as peculiar. He was talking about people like Sunday who, instead of complaining and fretting, has used her time to inform and bless.

Peter acknowledges the darkness that doesn't seem to be vanishing. Yet these otherworldly (peculiar) people I know rejoice, have hope, encourage, and reach out to others, trust, and persevere "as seeing him who is invisible" (Hebrews 11:27 ESV).

Reflections

There are a number of references in Scripture to Nazarites, people who intentionally were separated for service and devotion to the Lord. Samuel was one who was greatly used by God in the leadership and formation of the nation of Israel. John the Baptist also lived the life of a Nazarite, and he "prepared the way of the Lord" (Mark 1:3 NIV). Does the idea of being set apart to or for God seem difficult or even frightening? If so, how?

_____

_____

_____

Could Christians be termed nonconformists?

_____

_____

How does this apply or not?

_____

_____

Define a Christian in this twenty-first century.

_____

_____

Father, as you shape us, make us unique in the sense that we are your hands and feet, joyously anticipating how we may serve you by serving others. In Jesus's name. Amen.

PEACEMAKERS

Blessed are the peacemakers, for they will be called children of God.

—Matthew 5:9 (NIV)

I knew a wise woman who was full of homespun insight. She was an avid student of Christian literature, and she put into practice what she learned. A number of young women were often at her doorstep or on the phone seeking her advice.

She shared a story about a tiff she'd had with her husband. Apparently, neither of them wanted to concede a point and neither wanted to surrender. The stalemate seemed insurmountable since they were both strong-minded and convinced of their opinions.

But to this impasse the Holy Spirit spoke in her heart. "Share some of the mints you're eating," was the simple directive, which implied reaching out across the firing line. Initially she resisted, but the sweet voice continued and was insistent. Finally, she obeyed, and the battle was ended. Just like that.

The wise woman told me that pride and the insistence on always winning and being right can bring sustained grief to any relationship. Humbling oneself can be as easy as extending an olive branch (or mint) to our opponent and then watching God bring down the barriers. Yes, we often have to be first responders.

She went on to say that we are sometimes our greatest enemy in life and relationships. When Christ is our center, all other issues are peripheral, and we can live in peace. She wondered how many battles we lose by refusing to make peace and maintaining a *winning is everything* attitude rather than surrendering to God's kingdom orientation?

My friend told me that the more we listen and obey, the more consistently we experience God's joy and his life. Moreover, God's joy is one of those fruits of the Spirit that grows in a heart that lives and moves and has its being in him.

Reflection

When Jesus preached the Sermon on the Mount, there is only one thing he left out. He didn't mention that without him we could do nothing (John 15:5), which was part of another teaching time. We may have good intentions, but we forget that unless empowered by God, we can't keep the commandments or make peace or do any of his directives. If it is God's will in a circumstance, he can and will provide the means by which we can obey.

Peacemaking requires humility and a willingness to see one's part in conflict. It takes death to self (Luke 9:23-25), but we can do all things through Christ who strengthens us (Philippians 4:13). If he wills it, we can do it.

Think of a situation where you might be used as a peacemaker. Write a prayer asking God to work through you in obedience to his Word.

_____

_____

_____

Lord, thank you for nurturing us through fellow travelers who love you and willingly follow even when it means losing for the time being. Help us to be peacemakers, true children of God. Amen.

SEEING JESUS

Man looketh on the outward appearance, but the
Lord looketh on the heart.

—1 Samuel 16:7 (KJV)

An amusing story is told of a visit TE Lawrence,[22] the famed
Lawrence of Arabia, paid to his good friend, poet and novelist
Thomas Hardy. At the time, Lawrence was serving in the Royal Air
Force and was dressed in uniform when he showed up at Hardy's
house for tea. The mayoress of the village also happened to be a guest
and was horrified to be in the company of a common soldier.

The mayoress looked over at Mrs. Hardy, addressing her in
French, and said she'd never in all her life had to sit down to tea with
a private soldier. No one said a word.

Finally, Lawrence spoke with grace to the mayoress in perfect
French, saying, "I beg your pardon, madam, but can I be of any use
as an interpreter? Mrs. Hardy knows no French."

Oops. Are we ever guilty of looking at people and forming
judgments based on what we see rather than waiting to see who they
really are? Many people in Jesus's day did just that. They didn't wait
to see what was behind the humble man with calloused hands who
called sinners and publicans friends. They didn't take time to learn
who Jesus was.

Reflection

Did you hear about the pastor who dressed as a homeless man and showed up at his parish on Sunday morning? Most of his church members ignored or outright rejected him. He didn't fit into the parish profile. Later, when he came in and removed his costume, many were horrified at their behavior; others were angry at being unmasked.

How do you respond to someone unlike you?

_____

_____

_____

Jesus had compassion on the marginalized, forgave the sinners, challenged the religionists, and showed us how to live. What aspect of Jesus's character would you most want to emulate?

_____

_____

_____

What will you do to become more like Jesus?

_____

_____

_____

Lord, open my eyes so that I see the people you created behind the shapes they inhabit. Give me a heart to love, serve, and touch all those you bring to me. Remind me that you love me, warts and all, and help me do the same with others. In Jesus's name. Amen.

HIGHER GROUND

This one thing I do, forgetting those things which are behind, and reaching forth unto those things which are before, I press toward the mark for the prize of the high calling of God in Christ Jesus.
—Philippians 3:13–14 (KJV)

My friend Moses was a beautiful man, inside and out. I attended his graduation from Uganda Christian University in Mokono where he was president of the student council, class president, and outstanding male student. When he came to the United States for further study, we stayed in touch by phone, and then Moses returned to Uganda for a time of fruitful ministry.

A few years later, while I was preparing for a visit to Uganda, I received a message that Moses had died suddenly of an aneurism. I would just be able to get to his village in time for the burial service.

Members of Parliament stood to remember Moses's contributions to the community and nation; a former teacher spoke; and the archbishop delivered a powerful message. Then, the audience hushed as Moses's father, a retired bishop, stood to speak. The dear saint quietly thanked everyone for coming and was the soul of grace. And then he began to sing *a cappella* in his native tongue.

I recognized the tune from childhood:

"Higher Ground"
by Johnson Oatman Jr.
I'm pressing on the upward way,
New heights I'm gaining ev'ry day;
Still praying as I'm onward bound,
"Lord, plant my feet on higher ground."

"Lord, lift me up and let me stand
By faith, on heaven's tableland;
A higher plane than I have found,
Lord, plant my feet on higher ground.

That precious father went on to sing every verse, a prayer to *his* Father, who had never forsaken or disappointed him. He had lived his life daily abiding in God, trusting him for every need. When the ultimate test came, by faith he was able to turn his mourning into a hymn of praise.

Reflection

Another father, Horatio Spafford,[23] known to the world because of his powerful hymn "It Is Well with My Soul," also discovered peace in suffering. After losing a son to scarlet fever, the Chicago fire wiped out most of his assets. He was to join his wife and daughters in Europe for a holiday, when he received a cable: "Saved alone." An accident at sea cost the Spaffords their four daughters.

As Spafford crossed the sea to meet his wife, he asked the captain to notify him when they were at the spot where his daughters had perished. Prompted by faith, Spafford was inspired to write the words that still bring comfort to hearts today. One is especially touched with the line, "Whatever my lot, thou hast taught me to say, 'It is well, it is well with my soul.'"

One of the titles of the Holy Spirit is Comforter. When have you experienced comfort from the Holy Spirit?

_____

_____

Father, we want to know you intimately, feel your comfort supremely, and love you deeply so that in our times of severe testing, you are glorified in us. In Jesus's name. Amen.

LEADERS

Don't let anyone look down on you because you
are young, but set an example for the believers in
speech, in conduct, in love, in faith, and in purity.
                                        —1 Timothy 4:12 (NIV)

H ave you learned to be careful what you say around children?
Their hearing is remarkable, and their memory is even more
astonishing.

I have two friends who are missionaries in Kenya. They have
taught their two boys by example to love the Lord and to be obedient
to his teachings. Now they have two little disciples who diligently
live out the Gospel in their daily routines.

Matthew is seven years old and is enrolled with his brother in a
local public school. One day during the lesson, his teacher became
frustrated with one of the students and finally said to him, "You are
stupid."

At this, Matthew stood and courageously told the teacher that
she had said a bad word when speaking to his friend. I imagine
the teacher, already flustered, was further upset when Matthew
continued. "You should apologize to this boy and ask his forgiveness
for calling him a bad name."

When the teacher saw Matthew's intensity, she asked the student
to forgive her. She said that Matthew was right and then suggested
to the class that this event not be repeated to anyone.

Of course, that was not to be with a group of second graders.
Matthew went home and told his parents about the disturbance
in his classroom, and the following day, my friends went to visit
the teacher. They explained that they were entrusting their sons to
the teachers for the majority of the day and expected the teachers

to be examples. They knew the teacher had asked forgiveness, and they assured her that they also had forgiven her but reinforced the importance of her role modeling to all her students.

When I heard the story, and knowing Matthew and his brother as I do, I reflected on my own parenting (and grandparenting), even my own personal witness. How bold am I, how bold are my children and grandchildren in standing for truth? Is truth so important that I confront error when I see it, or do I tolerate unkindness or injustice rather than expect accountability? And how consistent is my life? Do my words reinforce what I try to live out every day? Matthew was bold when he stood up to point out what he saw was hurtful and bad, but he was also willing to take the consequences for his public witness.

Isaiah 11:6 says, "A little child shall lead them" (NKJV). May our daily lives consistently model Christ so that our children may indeed become leaders of their generation.

Reflection

If you were arrested for being a Christian, would there be enough evidence to convict you? This old challenge is still true today. Do people see the marks of Christ on us?

I once asked an assembly of Christian university teachers if they could be witnesses in a hostile environment without speaking. In an audience of more than three hundred student teachers, not one person raised a hand. How would you respond?

_____

_____

This quote falsely attributed to St. Francis reminds us to "Preach the Gospel at all times. Use words if necessary."[24] Do you agree or disagree with this premise? If yes, why? If no, why not?

_____

_____

Lord, make my family and me such lovers of Jesus who is Truth, that our lives reflect truth and that our mouths respectfully confront error. In Jesus's name. Amen.

THE LITTLE GUY

> One of the disciples—it was Andrew, brother to
> Simon Peter—said, "There's a little boy here who
> has five barley loaves and two fish. But that's a drop
> in the bucket for a crowd like this."
> —John 6:8–9 (MSG)

I've never heard anyone commend the little boy who brought the substantial lunch that fed thousands of Jesus's hungry followers. In fact, his name isn't even mentioned. We know about Andrew, who always quietly works in the background, and we know about Andrew's brash brother, Peter, who usually dominates the scene. But of the little boy who is instrumental in one of Jesus's major miracles, we read one sentence.

However, that single sentence tells us several things about this child through whom God worked:

1. He was young. Quite likely, this was a small child—a little boy, a boy, or a lad—as described by most versions. We don't know if he came alone or if he was with his family or hanging out with friends.
2. For whatever reason, he came to hear Jesus, and, as a result, took part in one of Jesus's most famous miracles simply because *he was present.*
3. He was probably poor (barley loaves were eaten by the poor). Although there may have been wealthier, more prominent people in the crowd, this small boy had exactly what Jesus needed to feed the thousands.
4. He was planning to share. What small boy would carry such a big lunch unless he was thinking of splitting it

with someone? Did this little guy come up to Andrew and volunteer his lunch when he saw the problem? Or did Andrew notice that the child had brought more than he needed?

There are so many details we don't know, but we do know that Jesus used a small, obscure, poor, unnamed, and generous young one to accomplish a great miracle that people still talk about today. The glory went to Jesus, and the little boy was merely an instrument but a powerful one at that.

Reflection

The story is told of Henry Morrison[25] and his wife on their return to the states after faithfully serving many years on the mission field. They didn't realize President Teddy Roosevelt was on the same ship.

As they neared port, they saw the massive crowds and bands playing. Morrison turned to his wife and said with gratitude, "They haven't forgotten us." When he realized his mistake, he was heartbroken.

Several days passed as the missionary rehashed his ministry and the lack of acknowledgement of hard-spent years in obscurity. His grief finally became unbearable; he did what he had done for a lifetime: he knelt and took his sorrow to God. As he poured out his bitterness in prayer, God spoke peace to his troubled heart with only a few simple words. "Henry, you're not home yet."

Does it ever seem that no one notices the sacrifices or energy you expend for Christ?

_____

_____

_____

_____

What does Jesus say in response to our service for him? (Matthew 25:40–45)

_____

_____

_____

How would you rewrite the following passage: "Take up [your] cross and follow me." (Matthew 16:24 NIV)

_____

_____

_____

Meditate on what following Jesus means. Ask yourself what discipleship entails.

Father, as I contemplate your way, help me to remember the awful cost you paid to be my Savior. Amen.

GENEROSITY

Give, and it will be given to you. A good measure, pressed down, shaken together and running over, will be poured into your lap. For with the measure you use, it will be measured to you.

—Luke 6:38 (NIV)

Having a treasury of grandchildren, I love to observe their intuitive understanding. Take William, for instance. He has been working with his dad on a miniature car for the Cub Scout derby race. Chris and William have selected and carved out the design, gotten the wheels, added weights to balance the machine, and checked to be certain the results of their hard work meet specifications.

In the middle of this intense activity, William was visiting and asked me if he could type a note to his friend. I set William up with paper, helped him align it on the typewriter, and he began to write, "Dear David. We need to make a play date. I hope you win the derby." With all his efforts, young William was wishing his friend would win.

Then there was the occurrence at children's chapel. The children are taught to give with offerings taken in their services. At collection time, William remembered that his dad hadn't given him any change.

He told his friend about the problem, and his buddy quickly resolved the dilemma. "Don't worry, William," he said. "My dad gave me a dollar." And with that, he proceeded to tear his dollar in two and gave one half to William.

That's what children are like. They're generous.

Reflection

On the mountain, Jesus said, "Blessed are the pure in heart, for they will see God" (Matthew 5:8 NIV)

Jesus told us to be like children, not childish, but pure in heart, trusting that our Father spoke truth and did everything he promised. And that he expected us to do everything he asked us to do—like giving. He even told us how much: "A good measure, pressed down, shaken together and running over" (Luke 6:38 NIV).

Little children are generous by nature because they know there's more where that came from. And we should have the same trust. Our Father knows what we need even before we ask (Matthew 6:8).

When have you been delighted with a gift from your heavenly Father?

_____

_____

Describe a time when gift-giving was a special treat:

_____

_____

What principle informs your giving?

_____

_____

_____

What did you hear in the stories of the little boys?

_____

_____

_____

Father, help us to free ourselves from the selfishness that makes us hold on to our stuff and those things that keep us from being like Jesus, who gave his all. Amen.

GIFTS

> There are different kinds of gifts, but the same
> Spirit distributes them. There are different kinds of
> service, but the same Lord. There are different kinds
> of working, but in all of them and in everyone it is
> the same God at work.
>
> —1 Corinthians 12:4–6 (NIV)

One of my favorite children's books is *Frederick*,[26] Leo Leonni's story of a little field mouse who might be perceived as a lazy do-nothing. Throughout the summer, all the other mice toiled diligently, preparing for winter, gathering food and storing it to sustain themselves through those long months. But as Frederick's friends pass him by carrying heavy loads of grain, he peacefully sits on a rock looking about, absorbing the rays of the sun. Frederick suggests that he too is preparing for winter, although his efforts are not obvious to anyone else.

After months of hard work, the fierce winter and cold winds drive the little mouse community into their underground refuge. Stashes of seeds and grains are brought out, and everyone shares.

Eventually, someone says, "Frederick, what did you gather for the dark winter days?"

And little Frederick, whose dreamy eyes have baffled them all, describes the marvelous colors and sights he has gathered, the wonderful words, and he paints love pictures of the sun and nature's beauty all around. As he speaks, the grayness of the long winter dissipates, and his poetry carries them through the harsh reality of the season.

We too need to identify the Fredericks among us. They are those who, no matter how difficult the circumstance, can be depended upon to remind us to think about and remember those things that are beautiful, pure, true, and honest. They remind us of God's promises and his presence with us. They may not always be in the forefront of the latest project or community volunteer program, but they're watching all the time and storing up God's faithfulness to remind us during dark days.

Each of us has a gift for God's kingdom. There are worker bees and those who are readily noticed for their energies, but there are also Fredericks who take time to sit, meditate, wait, and watch God at work. We need those Fredericks who, in our winter days, lift our spirits to see, hear, and remember God's goodness.

Reflection

I remember a particular mission trip that taught us all so much. We like to encourage anyone who feels called to come and go with us. The volunteers who showed up for this particular trip were, however, a bit unusual for mission.

Sherry, a lovely, gracious lady said she felt that she should be part of the mission but was unsure how she could fit in. As we talked further, I learned that Sherry was an interior designer. Quite frankly, I couldn't see what role she could take in this mission to Cuernavaca. We rarely need decorators in the marginalized places in which we work, but Sherry seemed called.

Patsy, a vivacious, petite woman, was equally enthusiastic. She too knew that she was to be part of the team. Patsy was an artist. Again, I was curious to see how God would use her gifts in the mission.

I should have been at ease all along. When the team arrived, they learned that they were to refurbish and decorate the community center. Sherry assisted with design and chose all the colors and fabrics, while Patsy painted lovely folk art designs around all the arched windows and doors. As a team, they were the perfect complement to the worker bees.

Have you discovered what gifts God has lavished on you?

_____

If not, spend time in prayer asking God to identify how your talent can be used for his glory.

Father, thank you for those in our lives who share your beauty, mercy, love, grace, and all things that cheer us onward. Help us to be generous with what you've given us. In Jesus's name. Amen.

SONS OF GOD

> But as many as received him, to them gave he
> power to become the sons of God, even to them
> that believe on his name.
>
> —John 1:12 (KJV)

LaRhesa and her team were commissioned to go to a Latin American country to build a house. When they arrived at the site marked by a rather large, verdant tree, they spied a pitiful little shack pieced together with boards and bits of tin.

The family slowly emerged to greet the team, but the father held everyone's attention. While the mother and children shyly smiled and nodded, the rather large man holding a machete glared belligerently at the visitors and stalked off to the fields.

The team worked through muggy tropical days to construct a new home for the hopeful family. Each day was the same: the crew arrived just after sunrise, and the children and mother would appear with warm welcomes. An unhappy father would march out his door, machete in hand, and make his way to the fields.

As the house was nearing completion, the team talked often among themselves, wondering at the lack of thanksgiving. LaRhesa reminded them that their mission was to help the family and to glorify God. Still ... the missioners finished and dedicated the little house, gave the family a Bible, and said goodbye.

Several years later, the church commissioned the team to build another house in the same region. On their way to the new site, someone suggested they check on the house they had built on their last trip. As they approached the location, the van made several runs by what they thought was the building site, but something didn't seem quite right.

There was the large tree, and they thought they recognized the house, but there was a big building on the other side of the tree that hadn't been there before. Everyone piled out of the van to explore.

A man came out of the big building with a huge smile on his face, and some of the team thought they recognized him. Could that be the angry father they had left? No, they decided, this man definitely looked younger. Finally, they approached the stranger, and he told them this story.

He was the man they encountered on their first mission, and he had been upset because he questioned their motivation. Why would someone build a house for a stranger? And without cost?

After the team left, he picked up the Bible and began reading. As he read, his heart changed, and he became a Christian. He grew and was transformed and became a pastor. He was so excited at the change in his life that he built a church, the large building standing next to the tree. And every week, people from nearby villages come to hear the Good News that was proclaimed when a team came to build a house.

Reflection

What parts of this story stand out to you?

_____

Have you ever done something for someone who never expressed gratitude or recognized your efforts?

_____

How did you react?

_____

_____

In your own words, write what Jesus is saying in Matthew 25:40, "Whatever you did for one of the least of these brothers and sisters of mine, you did for me" (NIV).

_____

_____

Thank you, Father, for trusting us to do your work without thought of reward. Amen.

ON THE ROAD

5

ON THE ROAD

It's time to move. We've made the decision to go, to look beyond
the Ranges. We will walk on this path that has lured so many
through the ages. And we're finding treasures we could not have
expected before we actually began the trek. We're meeting saints;
riddles are being unwound; and surprises of bounty meet us in
crooked places. A majestic lion speaks of love; a bishop entreats his
people to pray for their enemies; the persecuted Church survives
even through flames; and the Holy Spirit companions us.
What are you learning on your journey? Have
you invited anyone to go with you?

THE CROWD I CAN'T WAIT TO BE STUCK IN

> After this I looked, and there before me was a great multitude that no one could count, from every nation, tribe, people, and language, standing before the throne and before the Lamb. They were wearing white robes and were holding palm branches in their hands.
>
> —Revelation 7:9 (NIV)

One of our faithful missionaries and his family has served Christ in the Philippines for many years. Despite a serious medical condition, George and his wife engaged in intense study of the Tagalog language and the culture of the people to whom they would be ministering. After a long period of preparation, they headed for the jungles in a remote area of the island chain. They were in the bush for only a short time when they were airlifted to safety due to incoming terrorists. Once the danger was passed, George and Ginny returned to continue their ministry of love and compassion.

Later, this missionary couple became language specialists and worked closely with the indigenous folks and the missionaries living among them. The Philippines became home for all the family. In fact, when they returned to the United States on furlough, their youngest daughter pined for home, back to the Philippines. Embracing the call had totally captured their hearts.

George recently sent this beautiful reflection:

> I live in a very crowded city, Manila, the densest city in the world. What would normally be a fifteen-minute drive in the USA can take up to six hours

here on account of so many cars. People get irritated, and it is hot.

All around me are represented the 180 or so languages that exist in the Philippines. One day there will be people from every one of these languages standing among the great multitude, offering praise in their language to our Father. That is why I came here, to be stuck in this crowd for now so that one day they can join us before the Father in a much bigger crowd and with way more than 180 languages praising God.

On that day, we won't be irritated at the tightness of the crowd but will rejoice that we have all been forgiven, redeemed, and can stand in his glory before the throne. I think I will stand in the Filipino section.

Jesus said that his yoke is easy and his burden light (Matthew 11:30). As George and his family have embraced God's call on their lives, they have become not just comfortable in their adopted home, but the Filipinos have taken up residency in their hearts.

Reflection

How would you describe your spiritual home?

_____

_____

Who are those who have most shaped your life and fostered your growth in faith?

_____

_____

Name those who have become "family" through your Christian endeavors.

_____

_____

Thank you, Father, for your love that reaches the whole world. May I reflect that in my life. Amen.

A STRANGE MANDATE

> Seek the welfare of the city where I have sent you
> into exile, and pray to the Lord on its behalf; for in
> its welfare you will find your welfare.
> —Jeremiah 29:7 (ESV)

How do you tell Christians living in the middle of severe persecution and repression to pray for the perpetrators? Well, that's exactly what The Right Reverend John, former archbishop of Singapore, told his thousands of parishioners who live in Singapore, Indonesia, Cambodia, Laos, Nepal, Vietnam, and Thailand. Some of those countries are on the Open Doors *World Watch List*[27] for severe persecution of Christians.

When I questioned Archbishop John about this strange mandate, he reminded me of the context of this verse penned by Jeremiah. Thousands of years ago, the Old Testament prophet Jeremiah warned the people of Judah of impending disaster if they continued to disregard God and his laws. In spite of repeated warnings from numerous men of God, the people continued to follow their own desires, worshiping images, abusing the poor, sacrificing their own children to brazen idols, and turning their backs on God. Finally, they were taken into captivity in Babylon. Many would never return to their homes.

Yet it was to these very exiles that Jeremiah wrote the words that persecuted Christians in Archbishop John's churches would also be given. Both understood that God's grace was abundant and that he would sustain them through their prayers and repentance. "In its welfare you will have welfare" (Jeremiah 29:7 ESV) reminded them that nations and communities at peace are more likely to benefit the people than those experiencing deprivation, violence, or unrest.

Paul took this a step further when he admonished Timothy to "pray for rulers and for all who have authority. Pray for these leaders so that we can live quiet and peaceful lives—lives full of devotion to God and respect for him" (1 Timothy 2:2 Easy-to-Read Version). He didn't put any stipulations on the prayers such as to pray for good rulers or pray for the rulers you like.

The likelihood of making this journey with pilgrims from many other countries and life experiences is great in a time of global migration. With 24/7 communication networks, we are connected to brothers and sisters in real time who live in exile or hostile environments of war. Our prayers connect us not only to one another, but to the one who oversees our welfare and gives us his peace.

Reflection

Have you ever considered the newspaper, internet, or TV news reports as opportunities to reach out to those places that may need your instant intercessions? Never before have we been able immediately to thrust ourselves into conflict or persecution and ask for divine intervention. Or to ask for mercy or grace or justice. Let us not waste these marvelous gifts of technology to become the conduits for God's presence in obscure places of great need.

List some troubled areas in our world where God has touched your heart to pray:

_____

_____

Do some background research on these places to learn about the rulers and the issues. Then begin to pray specifically for those people and those issues. A wonderful book, _Operation World_ by Jason Mandryk,[28] lists the countries of the world and their needs. This is an excellent aid for your intercessions.

Father, all the leaders of the world bear heavy burdens. Work your will, your peace, and your love in their hearts. Fill them with your wisdom to govern that we may all live in peace and bring glory to your name. In Jesus our Lord. Amen.

AN APPEAL

But to you who are listening I say: Love your
enemies, do good to those who hate you, bless those
who curse you, pray for those who mistreat you.

—Luke 6:27–28 (NIV)

On the narrow pathway, we are asked to pray for one another.
Occasionally, we are compelled to intercede for those in real
peril. This appeal reached me from a young woman[29] caught in her
war-torn homeland that is the focus of the whole world. I watch,
grieved at her anguish and valiant determination to maintain her
identity as God's child. Although she may be thousands of miles
away, she is still my sister in Christ, and she asks me to pray.

"I realize quite well watching evil, even from a distance, corrupts
your soul," she writes. "I never had such anger. I never was that
disgusted with humankind. Then I zoom out and go back to my
Savior. I need him more than ever. The pain is real, the bloodshed
is real, the loss is real, and the injustice is real. My heart turns cold.
Love grows cold. I understand [the] text more than ever before. I
need Jesus, not to lose his image and not to take [the] role of a judge
because he is, and I am not.

"Lord, have mercy on me, on my country, on my people. We
all need that.

"The only thing is to continue to help others, be that Samaritan
so compassion would fill my heart, remove the self-righteous[ness]
and desire for revenge.

"I don't know who of you are praying for me, guys, but your
prayers are working ... one can't have sanity being that angry ...
thank you."

Often we are tempted to ask, "Where is God in the middle of suffering? Where is he when the young and the innocent perish? A friend said that he is there in the thousands who open their doors to refugees; he is there with the volunteers who prepare hot meals while shelling brings devastation to their villages; he is there with this Samaritan who prays and reaches out in love all the while battling the anger in her own heart. Someone else said, "God is just where he was when he watched his Son die on the cross."

We may not understand God's ways, but he implores us to trust that, in his time, his unfathomable love will work all things together for good.

Reflection

Martin Luther said that when we pray, we lay the need before God but do not prescribe to God a measure, manner, time, or place for his answer. That takes trust in his sovereignty and love.

How do you approach God in your prayers?

_____

_____

What do you think Jesus meant when he told the parable of the unjust judge in Luke 18?

_____

_____

Is Jesus inferring that God is unjust?

_____

_____

Father, please be with those who suffer. Pour your grace and mercy on them, and help us not to forget to pray. In Jesus's name. Amen.

THE CHURCH LIVES ON

On this rock I will build my church, and the gates
of hell shall not prevail against it.
>   —Matthew 16:18 (ESV)

The Church is alive and well. That is what I discover in my travels to places of dire poverty, in areas of severe persecution, and where governments are highly restrictive.

On my latest visit to see the Church in action, I observed a tiny country that has literally been shut off from the world for years. In a setting of breathtaking beauty, they have few outside resources and have felt themselves isolated. Even their lines of communication have been filtered coming and going. So what has happened to the Church in the meantime?

The people have learned to lean on God and each other. They have reached inside to develop their creativity and have trusted God rather than organizations and institutions to provide their needs. Moreover, they have found God to be faithful.

In a number of locations, hurricanes have blown down the buildings. Undeterred, parishioners have continued to meet in shelters, in homes, and in any place they could gather to worship and praise. They have patched up damaged chapels, and the Church has survived even when Mother Nature has dispatched the buildings.

In one parish, someone accused the pastor of a heinous crime, which was later proved untrue. Prior to his exoneration, his shame was so great that he took his own life. He perished singing a hymn.

Twelve young girls were so moved; they surrounded the altar in their sanctuary and pledged never to let the Church die. Then they opened the doors and invited everyone in for a celebration of the pastor's life and the life of the Church. More than eighty years later, the remaining "girls" continue to honor their pledge.

In another country where a revolutionary government fought to obliterate the Church, the Body went underground refusing to be destroyed. Bibles were confiscated, believers were tortured and imprisoned, and buildings were demolished. Today in that same country, Bibles are freely distributed as the Church has come out of hiding, and people worship freely.

Jesus said that no power could destroy the Church. Even as people suffer and must meet secretly, the Church remains.

Reflection

Can you recall eras in history where believers met in secret?

_____

_____

Are you aware of countries today that disallow Christians to worship freely?

_____

_____

To learn more about the struggles of persecuted Christians and how they can be supported, see https://www.opendoorsusa.org/, a nondenominational Christian organization.

Father, how humbled we are to see the faithfulness of your people around the world who serve you at great cost. Encourage and support them now and forever. In Jesus, our Lord. Amen.

JUST DO IT

And now these three remain: faith, hope, and love.
But the greatest of these is love.

—1 Corinthians 13:13 (NIV)

I heard a pastor say he had gotten up to preach, read his text, "Love one another," and then sat down. In the seconds it took to perform this action, a thousand discouraging thoughts went through his mind—things like, *nobody pays a bit of attention to the sermons, nobody cares, nobody does the sermons, what's the use.* He was ready to quit. He got up again and repeated his text. And he sat down. This happened three times.

After intense minutes of watching a church full of now-uncomfortable people squirming in their seats, looking around, wondering what to do, he noticed one person leaning over to talk to his seatmate. Then someone else got up to speak to another person across the aisle. People began weeping as conversations of reconciliation, forgiveness, and love broke out. The people began to do the sermon.

This curious event was repeated the following Sunday. The confessing clergyman saw his own lack of faith and discouragement and decided to preach the same sermon. The words of the Gospel again began to penetrate hearts, and renewal with transformation became widespread in the congregation.

As the pastor and his fellowship began to embrace the Word, he declared that churches only need about four sermons a year: one for each quarter with the other Sundays being given to practicing the truths that were being taught. It was no surprise that the church began to grow exponentially as people learned to hear and to do.

In our parishes, homes, and communities, are we *doing* love? Have we given up unloving behaviors and attitudes? There really is no excuse for not loving when God gave everything to love us to himself.

Let us love one another.

Reflection

How much knowledge is stored and rusting in our heads from lack of use? I think of the many sermons we hear on any number of helpful topics that just molder away because they've never seemed significant. Or we don't put the information into practice since we have so many distractions.

Many of the old saints found they were strengthened by their daily spiritual practices and lifestyles of obedience. Athletes go through brutal exercises to prepare for their games, as do soldiers for war. We know tests and trials do and will come to each of us, and we are more successful through practicing spiritual disciplines.

Rewrite 2 Peter 1:5–7, keeping in mind that our life of faith is one of obedience and spiritual growth as we follow the leading of the Holy Spirit: "Make every effort to add to your faith goodness; and to goodness, knowledge; and to knowledge, self-control; and to self-control, perseverance; and to perseverance, godliness; and to godliness, mutual affection; and to mutual affection, love" (2 Peter 1:5–7 NIV).

_____

_____

_____

The passage continues with, "If you possess these qualities in increasing measure, they will keep you from being ineffective and unproductive in your knowledge of our Lord Jesus Christ" (2 Peter 1:8 NIV). Might there be any promptings of the Holy Spirit that you have put on the shelf waiting for a more convenient time or when you feel like it?

_____

_____

Reminder: Paul writes in 2 Corinthians 6:2 (KJV), "Now is the acceptable time." Don't wait to be obedient.

Father, we don't always behave as your loving children. We are sorry, and we ask your forgiveness. Fill us anew with your love, and love through us. In Jesus's name. Amen.

YESU ROMO

As for me, I shall behold your face in righteousness;
I will be satisfied with Your likeness when I awake.
—Psalm 17:15 (NASB)

Our diocese has had a decades-long relationship with Nebbi Diocese in northwest Uganda. At one point, I worked there six-and-a-half months on a project, and I return once or twice almost every year. Besides its breathtaking natural beauty, I love the people. They are kind and friendly, and they love Jesus.

In Nebbi, the people have a beautiful salutation when they greet one another. As they see each other on the road, one shouts, *"Pakabed ni Yesu,"* meaning *praise Jesus*. The other responds, *"Yesu romo,"* or *Jesus satisfies*. Isn't this a lovely way to greet one another? And the people live in that truth. Having few financial resources, the Christians of Nebbi have learned to embrace that reality.

During a conference in one of the villages, my friend Helen was asked to pray for an old gentleman who was experiencing back pains. Helen prayed but was unable to see him until much later. When they finally met again, Helen asked about his back. He looked at her in surprise, reminding her that she had prayed for him. Of course, he was better. The Nebbi folk trust Jesus and expect him to meet their daily needs, including healing aching backs.

In an environment where we live in abundance, I wonder if we know how much we really need Jesus. Do we realize how truly impoverished we are without him? St. Augustine seems to have been cognizant of the same truth, spoken in different words: "You have made us for yourself, O Lord, and our heart is restless until it rests in you."[30]

On my chair in my home library sits a beautiful pillow with the words embroidered in pastel threads, "Yesu romo." It was given me by a young friend and is a daily reminder that the only source of satisfaction is Jesus.

Reflection

Our market economy must constantly create needs that can only be satisfied with a new product—new fashions, new vehicles, new technology, and so on. If we're not happy with the latest cell phone, we know that it will be only months before a new model will be introduced.

Isn't it joyful to realize that in Christ we have everything we need for life and godliness (2 Peter 1:3)? There are some things that never go out of style, and those eternal possessions always fulfill.

What eternal gifts have you received from Christ that continue to satisfy?

_____

_____

_____

How would you explain the contentment you enjoy in Christ?

_____

_____

_____

Meditate on Psalm 16:11 (Amplified Bible, Classic Edition): "In your presence there is fullness of joy; at your right hand are pleasures forevermore."

Father, you open your hands wide and fill us with yourself. May we stop pursuing those things that only temporarily slake our thirst. Thank you for Jesus. Amen.

MAXIMUM SHARING

Freely you have received; freely give.
—Matthew 10:8 (NIV)

W hile it was still safe to travel to Haiti, my friend Dr. John was showing us around a small village composed of former tent city dwellers. The population had been given the opportunity to select modest homes with the stipulation that they would work and maintain the community. We walked through the village, visiting one and then another new homeowner, followed all the while by an exuberant group of small children.

Clusters of ladies were gathered on scattered front porches visiting and sewing. Many raced toward us to display the embroidery work they were doing. The sewing team had visited several weeks earlier, and the ladies were practicing the stitches they'd learned. The finished pieces would be sold, with proceeds returned to the one who had created them.

We stopped at a tiny cinderblock home with a little convenience store perched out front. Its owner had cobbled wooden poles and tarps together and marketed snacks and sweets.

John introduced us and made a show of pulling out his wallet. "Watch this," he said. Dr. John bought a single packet of cookies and handed it to a preschooler.

Silence and a kind of reverence enveloped the children. The little one, surrounded by numerous others, quietly opened the package as we waited expectantly. With the wrapper removed, she systematically began handing out cookies. One by one. Not bothering to keep any for herself.

John bought more cookies, and we watched the action repeated until not a single child was left out. *A little child shall lead them.*

With a hearts of generosity, everyone was blessed.

Who needs a cookie? Pass them around.

Reflection

Where do we learn generosity? It cannot be in contemporary culture.

Imagine being with Jesus as he began passing out bread and fish. Standing next to him, one couldn't ignore that there would never be enough to feed even a handful of those who had come to listen, much less several thousand. But it happened.

How will we ever be able to satiate the material and spiritual needs of our own communities and those to whom God sends us? Never through our own means. But if God is supplier, and we don't cling to the gift, the blessing is multiplied and passed on.

Try this exercise. Ask God to show you someone or some ministry who could be resourced by you, your gift, whether miniscule or large. "Do not despise these small beginnings, for the Lord rejoices to see the work begin" (Zechariah 4:10 NLT). Record your findings.

_____

Don't be discouraged. Ask God to multiply your gift and then thank him.

Father, as we offer our gifts we ask you to multiply them and to bless them for your glory. In Jesus's name. Amen.

LIMITATIONS

But to each one of us grace has been given as Christ
apportioned it.

—Ephesians 4:7 (NIV)

Only those who were truly intimate knew the difficult
circumstances of Elizabeth's marriage. Her husband was
demanding, often unreasonable, and extremely careful about money.
The grace-filled life that people saw on Sundays was surely due to
Elizabeth's Christ-centered life.

Jesus was her best friend, and she had learned to utilize difficulties
as vehicles for spiritual growth. The very discomforts that could have
crushed a soul were transformed instead into parables for the many
who sought her counsel and who turned to her for comfort in their
own trials.

There was a recurring grief, however, that burdened Elizabeth
for years. She anguished at Christmas or birthdays or occasions for
giving gifts. The parsimonious budget imposed on her didn't permit
her generous soul to give as she wanted.

Years of agonizing over this seemingly impossible constraint
finally led Elizabeth to do what she did so well. She prayed. She
asked God somehow to allow her to give abundantly from her heart.
And then an idea came. Elizabeth thought of all the fabric scraps she
had amassed from years of sewing, and she began crafting appliquéd
pictures. At first they were simple, but as her confidence grew and
her imagination was given free rein, her pictures became works
of art.

Cleverly, Elizabeth requested her husband to make frames for
her creations, and together their artistry became known and highly
desired in their community. Friends and family were hopeful they

would be among those receiving an Elizabeth picture. As her skills grew, Elizabeth was invited to teach in a local specialty shop, and her pieces soon were bringing in fees that she could never have imagined.

The limitation that initially had brought grief to Elizabeth was embraced and became the incentive for reaching inside to allow the inner beauty to be expressed through her art. While few people knew the pain that had been the impetus of her gift, everyone delighted in the joy she had wrung from her sorrow.

Reflection

What limitation or impediment seems to spoil the beauty of your days?

_____

_____

What creative actions have you taken to address your sense of limitation?

_____

_____

Purposefully, dedicate time in prayer for God's creative response, knowing that it may be, "My grace is sufficient for you, for my power is made perfect in weakness" (2 Corinthians 12:9 NIV).

Loving Father, thank you for transforming sorrow, pain, and suffering into things of beauty as we trust you to fill and use us for your dear purposes. May we, like the oyster, learn to embrace the irritants that they may become objects of beauty to your glory. In Jesus's name. Amen.

ABUNDANCE

> If you, then, though you are evil, know how to give
> good gifts to your children, how much more will
> your Father in heaven give good gifts to those who
> ask him!
>
> —Matthew 7:11 (NIV)

Our World Missions department is rarely stumped with the requests that come from our international partners, but when Mama Phoebe, the bishop's wife, asked if we could bring wedding dresses on our next visit, we were at a loss. "When girls in Uganda get married, they like to have white dresses, but they've very expensive. Can you help?" Phoebe entreated.

Our director, Betty, didn't hesitate. Immediately upon her return from overseas, Betty went from store to store pricing dresses that we could deliver to the expectant brides. It didn't take much shopping for her to realize that purchasing just a few dresses would exhaust our annual budget. So Betty did what we always do when a problem seems unsolvable. She prayed. "Lord," Betty implored, "there's no way we can afford these dresses, but you told us to ask, and so I'm asking for your assistance."

At the very next staff meeting, one of the bishops mentioned that he'd had a curious call. A parishioner wanted to close her bridal salon and needed to dispense with all the merchandise. Were we interested? Betty didn't hesitate.

Within a week Betty was called to the loading dock where a sixteen-wheeler was unloading cargo: bridal gowns; shoes; veils; prayer books; and bridesmaid, mother-of-the-bride, and mother-of-the-groom dresses. Everything and more than she had asked. In fact, after sorting out all the bounty, there was more than enough for our Ugandan friends *and* our Mexican friends. The Mexicans had enough merchandise to open their own bridal salons, and a church on the Mexican border purchased a van with the funds they received by selling their stock.

Anytime we begin to think that the need it too great or that it would be presumptuous to ask God to answer a frivolous request, we remind each other of the wedding dresses. We might have thought the appeal was ridiculous, but it was a glorious way for God to demonstrate his love and abundance.

Reflection

Occasionally, I hear someone say their request is so small or so odd or some such that they don't want to bother God. Perhaps, when Jesus mentions the needs of the birds of the air or the clothing of the lilies of the field (Matthew 6:26–30), he's referring to needs we may designate as trivial. How often do we stop to mend a child's toy or wipe a tear shed at a youngster's disappointment?

Have you ever experienced God's abundance? A time or event when his goodness surprised you? Describe that.

_____

_____

If we pray specifically, what may be the responses we receive?

_____

_____

Did you mention no, or wait?

_____

_____

Do those responses mean God doesn't answer prayer? Please explain.

_____

_____

Father, thank you for pouring out blessings on your undeserving servants. Give us faith to ask great things that you may be glorified. In Jesus's name. Amen.

LOVE ONE ANOTHER

My command is this: Love each other as I have
loved you.

                  —John 15:12 (NIV)

Sermons are all around us—if we have eyes to see and ears to hear.
The totality of Jesus's life was a seismic paradigm shift from the
letter to the spirit of the law. When he said, "Love one another," he
was pointing toward an internal work of the Spirit that would carry
believers beyond the obligatory going the first mile and perfunctory
forgiveness into abandoned display of God's love through us.

We saw a picture of unselfish love one twilight in Africa. I had
asked our guide if we could please see some lions, *a* lion. Every visitor
to an African game park wants to see a lion, and one is never satisfied
until this desire is fulfilled. No other animal has the majesty and
inherent magnificence than does the king of the beasts.

Hoping to oblige us, the guide directed our driver through miles
of dusty roads cut through the preserve, and then we stopped. Just in
front of our van, not even concerned about blending into the jungle
grasses, was a gorgeous male lion under a bush only yards from us.
His tail casually but effectually stretched across the path blocking
our further approach. In his golden aura, he silently surveyed his
kingdom and us.

Momentarily, a second lion, as splendid as the first, arrived, and
the lions nuzzled one another. Flaxen manes intermingled as we
were caught up in their touching display of affection. Their deep
connection to one another and their savannah home was obvious.

Four years ago, when park rangers found the first lion, his leg
had been caught in a poacher's cruel trap, and infection had already
gone to the bone. The resident vet determined that the leg had to be

amputated to save the lion's life. And so it was that the king of the jungle was no longer able to hunt or protect himself. But his brother appeared, and for *four years* his brother has walked with him and guarded him, and the females have brought him food.

We watched in silence. Loving one another. Even the animals understood. That is what we saw.

Reflection

Our faith communities call us to love one another, to bear the burdens of one another, and to look to the good of each other. When we love our neighbors as we love ourselves, we are loosed from the chains of self: hedonism, narcissism, egotism. Our cares are lighter because they are shared, and we see to the needs of each other.

How would you like to see your Christian community transformed?

_____

_____

What can you do to show Christ's love in tangible and practical ways?

_____

Ask God to show you one person to whom you can show his love.

_____

Father, you've told us that the animals will teach us. Open our eyes and our hearts so we may love just as you love us. In Jesus our Lord. Amen.

CHEERLEADERS

A new command I give you: Love one another. As I
have loved you, so you must love one another.
—John 13:35 (NIV)

William Carey, known as the father of modern missions in the eighteenth century, faithfully toiled, carrying the Gospel to India and translating the Bible into many Indian dialects. Carey was a social reformer who opened schools for poor children and crusaded to end the traditional practice of *sati* (a historical Hindu practice in which a widow sacrifices herself by sitting atop her deceased husband's funeral pyre). Additionally, William Carey opened one of India's first theological schools.

Many people are familiar with Carey's work, but few know of his sister, who was bedridden and unable to use her limbs for about fifty-two years. As Carey poured out his heart and concerns about the people with whom and to whom he daily ministered, his sister Polly prayed daily and maintained a vibrant correspondence by writing with a pencil in her mouth. Such was her love and commitment to her brother's calling.

Love is more than sentiment. At best, it is an action verb. Gary Chapman's book, *The 5 Love Languages*,[31] lists ways of showing love: affirming, touching, giving, serving, and spending time with the beloved. One can love without all the fuzzy emotions we sometimes equate with love by simply validating and affirming that other person, letting him or her know that he or she is special, cared for, thought about, and prayed for. And it's best done by getting ourselves out of the way so that we can focus on someone else.

Whom can we actively love today? How can we sacrificially give our time to build up someone? How can we, through God's love, leave our own cares and be cheerleaders for someone else? The cost is self-interest, but that begins to diminish as we get into the big world of *God's love.*

Let's find someone to love.

Reflection

I know someone who determined, after the death of her husband, that she would not spend valuable time in self-pity waiting for others to fill her voids. She began an active campaign inviting friends for tea or dinner and soon found that her invitations were returned. She then began looking around for people who had become disconnected from fellowship. Phone calls and notes followed, and soon the contacts morphed into delightful acquaintances and new friendships.

Look around. List the people within your church or neighborhood community who might appreciate or need your touch.

_____

_____

_____

Remember Jesus's words to us: "Whatever you did for one of the least of these brothers and sisters of mine, you did for me" (Matthew 25:40 NIV).

Father, give me creative ideas for encouraging, affirming, building up, and healing. I want to be a cheerleader. In Jesus's name. Amen.

ANGELS AND MORE ANGELS

The angel of the Lord encamps around those who
fear him, and he delivers them.

—Psalm 34:7 (NIV)

L aunching any mission trip is work. A lot of work. The logistics
of travel, accommodations, meals, and the project can take
months, even years.

A group of clergy had invited us to organize a conference for both
clergy and lay leaders, and we were finally ready for departure. Our
destination was a city where violence and destruction are everyday
happenings. Obviously, it was imperative that our mission *pray-ers*
at home interceded throughout our absence.

Travel day is always exhausting, but our gracious hosts met us
at the city's outskirts and escorted us through the twilight to the
place we'd be staying for the next several days. Imagine our surprise
and astonishment when we saw at least fifteen federal police vehicles
parked just in front of our hotel. Black and white never looked so
beautiful.

Registration proceeded quickly, and we paraded to a local
church where a fiesta was awaiting our arrival. Although I'd asked
if we might return to our hotel while the evening was still early,
something must have been left out of translation. Music, dance,
drama, and elaborate costumes filled the evening. And the meal
following was a feast. All the while, it got later.

How can I describe the tension of trusting God while the clock
hands kept moving? I am so grateful that God's ability does not rely
on our emotional states. We were in a situation where all we could
do was pray and trust. And of course, when the evening activities
were closed, our kind hosts shepherded us safely back to the hotel.

The next day during a break in sessions, I walked to the front entrance of our hotel, only to be greeted by banks of armed uniformed officers in the lobby. One of the clergy told me that during their morning assembly, the police had requested he stop and pray with them for *their* protection.

Not only did God send us the protection of angels in the form of police officers, but apparently, there was a multitude of angels guarding us waking and sleeping.

What a coincidence.

Reflection

The psalmist fills pages of scripture with intercession for safety. To many in the military Psalm 91 is the epic word on God's protection and care of his children. Congregations often pray these words over their parishioners in service for their country.

Can you describe an instance when you experienced God's protection?

_____

_____

_____

What is your favorite scripture verse regarding God's care?

_____

_____

_____

Thank you, Lord, for the wonderful ways in which you answer our prayers and for your protection. All honor be yours. Amen.

ABOUNDING GRACE

So let us come boldly to the throne of our gracious
God. There we will receive his mercy, and we will
find grace to help us when we need it most.

—Hebrews 4:16 (NLT)

P robably one of the most comforting thoughts we can have as we
go on mission is that we are sent by God. We're not out to do our
own thing, but we are servants of the Lord Jesus Christ, representing
him and our heavenly Father.

When I found myself stranded in Frankfurt on my way to
Russia, I had to remind myself that this was God's work and idea.
I had stood in line waiting to board a flight to Moscow when the
attendant told me I couldn't board. My visa had the wrong date on
it. Sure enough, having just completed a five-country tour, we had
inadvertently listed the wrong date for the visa application to Russia.

I searched for hours up and down Frankfurt's seemingly endless
airport for someone who could direct me to the Russian consulate
where I could get the date changed on my visa. I had no time to
get to Berlin and back. Surely there was a closer office. I spent the
night at a local hotel having sent calls flying between Frankfurt, San
Antonio, London, Yugoslavia, Russia, and back around the circuit.
And there were lots of prayers sent heavenward.

In the morning, my devotional reading began with, "And God
is able to make all grace abound toward you; that ye, always having
all sufficiency in all things, may abound to every good work" (2
Corinthians 9:8 KJV). I knew instantly that the visa represented a
huge need for God's abounding grace.

I ate breakfast and then asked the concierge to please call a cab.
When I entered the cab, I sensed that I should ask the driver to

please take me to the Russian Federation Consulate. (Why hadn't I thought of a cabbie earlier?) Arriving at the consulate, I was told to contact a colleague in Russia for a faxed letter of invitation to authorize a new visa. I placed a call to my friend in Russia, and the fax was sent almost immediately. My new friend at the consulate instructed me to pay the fee, and I was headed for the airport and my flight to Moscow.

When I left the states, I did not know that my visa was invalid or that there would be difficulty procuring one in Frankfurt. I could not have known the need for a letter of invitation or how to get it. I could not have known that it typically takes six weeks to get a new visa. I didn't know, but God did, and he provided abounding grace to meet every unanticipated need for his purposes and his glory.

Reflection

Have you ever beaten yourself about the head and shoulders because you made a stupid mistake?

_____

_____

And have you ever discovered that God can use even our mistakes?

_____

_____

Would this verse from 1 Corinthians have brought encouragement to you had you been in such a circumstance?

_____

_____

How does God's Word shape or direct your faith walk?

_____

_____

A good verse to memorize: "So then faith comes by hearing, and hearing by the word of God" (Romans 10:17 NIV).

Dearest Father, help us embrace humbling experiences as opportunities to see your glory. Help us trust you for your provisions when we've reached our dead ends. Thank you. In Jesus's name. Amen.

DIVINE APPOINTMENTS

In all thy ways acknowledge him, and he shall direct thy paths.

—Proverbs 3:6 (KJV)

In thinking about the various folks I've shared planes with, I always wonder who I will meet on upcoming flights. We have learned to pray for God's direction and divine appointments. While it's obvious that some passengers are heaven-sent, and others are, well, opportunities, I've had some memorable encounters.

Like the darling little girl who had obviously just seen the movie *Frozen*. We were serenaded with ditties for endless miles. You can guess her favorite: when she got to "Let It Go," she did. She sang *a voce alta*, with a *loud* voice.

But the passenger I won't forget was Aisha. After I missed my flight from Frankfurt to Moscow, I couldn't make an important meeting with Dr. Maria Tschernoskaya. God intervened, however, and I was enabled to catch an evening flight. I prayed that no one would sit near me so I could catch up on the work that had been neglected due to my delay. That prayer was not to be answered.

I tried to appear busy as the plane filled, and an attractive young lady sat one seat over. We exchanged polite greetings, and I turned back to my papers. But Aisha was not to be daunted. "What takes you to Moscow? What will you be doing?" Just what I wanted to avoid. I curtly answered her questions, adding that I was to have met with one of the foremost experts in care for orphans and vulnerable children.

Aisha listened quietly and then said, "I work with someone like that."

Mildly interested, I added, "This woman has a model project, and we were to meet to collaborate on a program for all of Eastern Europe."

After a moment, Aisha remarked, "The woman I work with also consults with many people who come to see her work in Moscow."

With piqued interest, I described our vision, and Aisha revealed that she was an Oxford professor who had come to work with—yes, Dr. Maria Tschernoskaya. Together they were developing methods that could be replicated in many former Soviet Union facilities.

Eating humble pie, I questioned Aisha, and for the remainder of the flight we exchanged notes while I wrote as fast as my hand could move. Aisha, with her command of the English language, was much more proficient in describing the program than Dr. Tschernoskaya ever could have been. Everything I'd planned to discuss with the noted expert was addressed in my evening with Aisha.

As the plane prepared to land, Aisha turned to me and said, "I wasn't supposed to be on this plane."

"Nor was I," I added.

Reflection

Occasionally, we wonder about God's failures—failure to understand, failure to care, failure to provide, failure to give us what we want, failure to answer prayer. Have you heard a country-western song called "Unanswered Prayers"[32] by Garth Brooks? The lyrics tell the story of a relationship that fell apart and ends with:

> Remember when you're talkin' to the man upstairs
> That just because he may not answer doesn't mean he don't care.
> Some of God's greatest gifts are unanswered.
>
> Some of God's greatest gifts are all too often unanswered.
> Some of God's greatest gifts are unanswered prayers.

It takes time to realize that *no* can be the key to God's higher response to our naïve prayers. Once we release God from our expectations, he is freed to do more than we can think or ask.

When did *no* turn into a better response than you'd originally anticipated?

_____

_____

_____

Write a thank you prayer for what you haven't yet received.

_____

_____

_____

Father, why am I often surprised at your loving ways? Thank you for always going before us and giving us what we need rather than what we think we want. Amen.

PILGRIMAGE

Whether you turn to the right or to the left, your
ears will hear a voice behind you, saying, "This is
the way; walk in it."

—Isaiah 30:21 (NIV)

Have you read *Pilgrim's Progress*[33] recently? That venerable tome
written by John Bunyan and published in the seventeenth
century can be credited to Bunyan's jail time in Bedford, England.
Apart from the Bible, *Pilgrim's Progress* has become the best-selling
book in publishing history. It's a story with episodes to which we
can all relate in our own spiritual ventures.

I love literary references to spiritual journeys, and in *Pilgrim's
Progress,* Christian leaves the City of Destruction for a perilous
journey to the Celestial City. As long as he follows his guides,
remembers the teachings, and holds to the path, he escapes the
dangers inherent along the way. When he becomes distracted, he
finds himself beset by any number of disturbances that cause him
great grief and, occasionally, great pain. Nevertheless, there is always
help for him.

Even though written hundreds of years ago, the path for pilgrims
seems remarkably similar. Distractions abound and temptations
surround us. Just as the pilgrim makes progress by keeping to the
path, by obeying the teachings, and by keeping his focus on the
Celestial City and the King, we can likewise successfully negotiate
the narrow way. We have a guide who can be trusted, and experience
teaches us the merits of listening to him rather than formulating our
own direction. Happily, we travel with a community of saints who
share the road and who can help us in our journey.

Wouldn't you like to become more astute in recognizing diversions and perils along the way? I love knowing that I'm not traveling alone and that so many others experience the same temptations and disruptions that plague me. Together, we can set our sights on the high calling in Christ Jesus who has promised always to be with us and to lead us safely home.

Take time to read (or reread) Bunyan's classic. It will affirm, encourage, and inspire you. And I'm certain you will identify with some of the characters and much of the journey. Along with Christian, let's journey onward to our Father's house in the Celestial City. There is joy, joy, joy.

Reflection

The path we travel is indeed straight and narrow but never so difficult that we do not always have our companion and guide with us. We walk by faith and not by sight (2 Corinthians 5:7) because that is enough. Emotions, faculties, and reasoning fail. But God is enough.

Paul's beautiful testimony in 2 Corinthians 4:7–10 (KJV) reads:

> But we have this treasure in earthen vessels,
> That the excellency of the power may be of God,
> And not of us.
> We are troubled on every side,
> Yet not distressed;
> We are perplexed,
> But not in despair;
> Persecuted, but not forsaken;
> Cast down,
> But not destroyed;
> Always bearing about in the body the dying of the Lord Jesus,
> That the life also of Jesus might be made manifest in our body.

What words of wisdom would you leave for those who are following?

_____

_____

Suggest three actions that will help others stay on the road to the Celestial City:

_____

_____

Father, thank you for those who have gone before us and who share their wisdom with those of us who follow. And thank you for those who have journeyed with me through the pages of this little volume. May we all continue to find joy as we travel together following Jesus. Amen.

ACKNOWLEDGMENTS

As is much of my life, this collection is a group project, and I am deeply grateful to a number of people who were part of its creation.

My son Christopher encouraged me to write a blog long before I'd heard of blogging. Since it wasn't part of my vernacular, I put the idea on a shelf. And then I met editor Jane Campbell when we were participating in a missions conference in rural Kenya. Jane seconded the suggestion about blogging. Thinking this might be a divine nudge, I acquiesced.

Marjorie George, beloved past director of communications for the Episcopal Diocese of West Texas, cornered me one day and said I needed to gather the blogs into a book. When the twenty-fifth anniversary of our World Missions department approached, it seemed an appropriate time to publish these stories along with other mission narratives.

Elizabeth Cauthorn, retired publisher and talented friend, provided excellent direction for the organization of materials, while Brenda Kingery, contemporary artist and founding member of Threads of Blessing International, collaborated with Barry Watson, graphic specialist, to style the artwork. Threads of Blessing members (a microenterprise in Uganda) created some of the tapestry pieces that we have gratefully used.

My patient colleague Catherine Markette spent hours reading and editing disparate pages. Stephen Little, attorney extraordinaire, mediated a computer glitch that had troubled me for days. Caroline Mowen, Canon to the Ordinary for DWTX, embraced the project from the beginning and had valuable suggestions.

A special thank you to other faithful missioners who shared their stories: Cookie Harrison, the Rev. Eric Fenton, the Rt. Rev. Jim Folts, Karen Lee, Brenda Kingery, the Rev. Justin Lindstrom, Edwina

Thomas, the Rev. Getahew Teshome, Maria Cavazos, Catherine Lillibridge, the Rev. Patrick Gahan, Betty Chumney, Sunday Dughira, LaRhesa Moon, George Olson, The Most Rev. John Chew, Dr. John Leininger, and my sweet children and grandchildren.

I am always grateful to our diocesan bishop, the Rt. Rev. David Reed, who never fails to support our ministries and is a constant source of encouragement.

Thank you all for the many hours you contributed to meetings, editing, suggestions, and encouragement. And thank you to the missioners of the Diocese of West Texas who faithfully persevere in loving and ministering to our many partners around the world.

I am grateful.

ENDNOTES

1   Cyril J. Davey, *Sadhu Sundar Singh.* (Waynesboro: STL Books, 1950), 52.

2   Wikipedia, *Saint Telemachus,* retrieved May 31, 2023, from en.m.wikipedia.org.

3   Elisabeth Elliot, *Keep A Quiet Heart* (Ann Arbor: Vine Books, 1995), 83.

4   Jeanne Guyon, *Madame Guyon: An Autobiography* (Chicago: Moody Press, n.d.).

5   EC Dawson, *Heroines of Missionary Adventure* (London: Seeley, Service & Co., Limited, 1930).

6   Steve Saint, *The Great Omission: Fulfilling Christ's Commission Completely* (Seattle: YWAM Publishing, 2001).

7   Brother Lawrence of the Resurrection, *The Practice of the Presence of God* (Garden City: Image Books, 1977).

8   Parish of St. Matthew with St. Paul, Winchester, *Pilgrims on a Journey,* retrieved May 31, 2023, from stmatthewstpaul.org.

9   CS Lewis, *Miracles* (New York: Macmillan Publishing Co., Inc., 1960).

10 *Book of Common Prayer* (New York: The Church Hymnal Corporation, 1979).

11 Oswald Chambers, *My Utmost for His Highest* (New York: Dodd, Mead & Company, Inc., 1935).

12 AJ Russell (ed.), *God Calling* (New York: Dodd, Mead & Company, Inc., 1978).

13 Samuel Bagster, *Daily Light on the Daily Path* (Grand Rapids: Daybreak Books, 1972).

14 Will Carleton, *Will Carleton Quotes,* retrieved June 2, 2023, from loveexpands.com.

15 Amy Carmichael, *Edges of His Ways* (Fort Washington: CLC Publications, 1955).

16 Norman Vincent Peale, *The Power of Positive Thinking* (Upper Saddle River: Prentice Hall, 1952).

17 Evelyn Underhill, Excerpts from *The Essentials of Mysticism.* In Richard J. Foster & James Bryan Smith (Eds.), *Devotional Classics* (San Francisco: HarperSanFrancisco, 1993), 114.

18 GK Chesterton, *The Really Complete "Father Brown" Mysteries,* Kindle ed., (G. Fisher, 2013), p. 426.

19 Leo Tolstoy, *Where Love Is, There God Is Also* (Nashville: Thomas Nelson Publishers, 1993).

20 David Adam, *Flame in My Heart* (London: Triangle, 1997), p. 67.

21 Eberhard Bethge (ed.), *Deitrich Bonhoeffer Letters & Papers from Prison* (New York: Touchstone), 1953.

22 Ronald D. Knight, *Colonel T. E. Lawrence Visits Mr. & Mrs. Thomas Hardy* (R. D. Knight), 1985.

23 Horatio Spafford. Retrieved June 2, 2023, from en.m.wikipedia.org.

24 Glenn Stanton. *FactChecker: Misquoting Francis of Assisi,* retrieved June 2, 2023, from thegospelcoalition.org.

25 *The Missionary's Return,* retrieved June 2, 2023, from addeigloriam.org.

26 Leo Lionni, *Frederick* (New York: Dragonfly Books, 1967).

27 Open Doors *World Watch List,* an annual ranking of the fifty countries where Christians face the most extreme persecution.

28 Jason Mandryk and Patrick Johnstone, *Operation World: The Definitive Prayer Guide* (Colorado Springs: Biblica Publishing, 2010).

29 Text message to TK, Life in a War Zone, March 10, 2022.

30 Augustine, *Confessions* (New York: The Modern Library, 2018), 3.

31 Gary Chapman, *The Five Love Languages* (Chicago: Northfield Publishing, 1992).

[32] Garth Brooks and Larry Bastian, "Unanswered Prayers" (song). On *No Fences* (Nashville: Capitol, 1990).

[33] John Bunyan, *The Pilgrim's Progress* (Gainesville, Florida: Bridge-Logos, 1998.

Printed in the United States
by Baker & Taylor Publisher Services